DISCOVER
BURNS BOG

by Bill Burns

Photography by Don DeMille

Hurricane Press

Vancouver, BC

Copyright © 1997 Bill Burns

All rights reserved. No part of this publication may be reproduced
or transmitted in any form or by any means without prior written
permission of the publisher, except by a reviewer who may quote
brief passages.

Published by
Hurricane Press
#406 - 119 West Pender Street
Vancouver, B.C.
Hurricane Press Canada V6B 1S5

Canadian Cataloguing in Publication Data

Burns, Bill, 1944 –
   Discover Burns Bog

Includes index.
ISBN 0-9698845-1-6

1. Burns Bog (B.C.) – Guidebooks.
2. Hiking – British Columbia – Burns Bog – Guidebooks.
3. Burns Bog (B.C.) – History. I. Title.
FC3845.B799B87 1997   917.11'33   C97-910985-X
F1089.B95B87 1997

Original artwork by Bill Burns
Photographs by Don DeMille (except where noted otherwise)
Proofreading by Robin Van Heck
Typesetting by Baseline Type and Graphics Cooperative

Printed in Canada by Hignell Book Printing

*Cover: A beautiful sandhill crane superimposed on a
yellow pond lily. Both are native species to the bog.
Photograph by Don DeMille*

Contents

Foreword

What Price Wilderness?

by David Bellamy

David Bellamy
Bill Burns photo.

 I first saw Burns Bog over 20 years ago while researching loca-
tions for part of a documentary series, called *Botanic Man,* which
was shown around the world. The particular episode centred on
the role of peatlands in unravelling history since the last bout
of global warming, which melted glaciers and permafrost and
allowed life to return to millions of hectares of Canada.

Burns Bog, the largest self-contained raised bog on the west coast of the
Americas, seemed an ideal subject for my research. Burns Bog is Vancouver's
own backyard wilderness, a nature reserve of international importance, as well
as an enormous carbon sink. It was also a solar-powered broadsheet without
equal, having chronicled all major local events, both natural and people-made,
since it began life some 5,000 years ago.

What an asset. And what a great film location, with superb hotels and
vibrant city life nearby. Perfect, but for one thing: Great machines were then at
work destroying the bog, carving the history book into sections and sucking up
its peaty pages to be bagged for sale. I went on my way with a heavy heart,
thinking that Burns Bog would, like so many other bogs I had seen, be erased
from the face of the living Earth and turned into just another tract of unreal
estate, so I chose another location to conduct my research.

In the intervening years I have been privileged to see a cross-section of the
world's peatlands. I returned to Burns Bog at the invitation of an amazing lady,
Eliza Olson, president of the Burns Bog Conservation Society. Part Cherokee,

part Hungarian, she now has become a champion of the cause of local conservation. There on the banks of the Fraser River—much changed since my last visit, its run of salmon much depleted by pollution and misuse—I witnessed what can only be described as a natural miracle. Those parts of the bog that had been mined for peat have begun to heal themselves. The sandhill cranes still dance their dance heralding another generation, the plants and animals both rare and common are there, and peat is still forming, doing its best to cool the brow of global warming and wafting nascent oxygen across the delta.

Sadly, the unreal estate is also there, the largest waste landfill west of Toronto, golf courses, cranberry monoculture, the creep of urban development and much more at the end of the planning pipelines that are draining the lifeblood of Burns Bog and so threatening the living world on which we all depend.

How could a great city plan for such desecration? If those plans are allowed to go ahead, a monument should be raised naming those who plan to profit from the despoliation of such a special feature of the landscape: a unique raised bog that has already fought back from the brink of extinction, a thing of immense value and lasting utility and beauty. As the people of Vancouver ponder the way ahead, they should remember that whatever their decision, the results can be seen from outer space. What an epitaph to their stupidity or good sense.

What price wilderness? What price a living history book covering so much of the history of people in this beautiful corner of the Earth? What price the dance of the sandhill cranes right in your own backyard? Burns Bog must be saved in its entirety and allowed to carry on doing the many important tasks it has performed for the past 5,000 years.

It is my honour to write a foreword to this superb book.

David Bellamy
Bedburn, England

Foreword

The Greatest
Teacher of All

by Dr. Richard Hebda

Dr. Richard Hebda

 Twenty-three years ago I arrived on the west coast of Canada to begin graduate studies at the University of British Columbia. I came to learn at the feet of the botanical masters about plants, their geography and ecology, and especially their ancient history. My graduate research project was to be the description of the origins and development of a bog, the Great Delta Bog, now widely known as Burns Bog.

Over the next three and a half years I stomped, stumbled and squished my way through this remarkable entity, observing and learning. I took peat cores to work out its origin and history from the study of sediments and plant remains. I recorded reams of notes on the exceptional plant communities and plant species. I digested this knowledge in the context of the wisdom taught by my university mentors and others who knew the bog. I was "educated."

But something else happened too. With each visit to the bog, I smelled and heard, I saw and touched and I began to understand, deep within, that something was communicating with me in an intuitive and profound way. Burns Bog was not a place simply to measure and record natural phenomena and test hypotheses and understand processes. It was a place with unique characteristics and a unique history, it was part of a natural legacy, with as much right to exist and right to a secure future as I had.

I even remember the day, wandering through the exotic haze of Labrador tea, when I finally understood the history and origins of the bog as I later described them in my thesis. It was an ecological symphony comprising land, water and life played out every day for no audience in particular, but for all to enjoy. As I came to understand the bog, I also came to realize that I had a responsibility for this entity, an entity which irreversibly shaped my future.

Over 5,000 years, plants, animals, atmosphere and land had, in an infinity of ways, converted a teeming estuary into marshes, then swamps, and finally into a distinct patch of biological diversity we know today as Burns Bog. Its environmental conditions and creatures differ so dramatically from the surrounding landscape that they add a quantum of biological diversity to the region, not just a species or two. Also, the bog's relatively distinct boundaries help illustrate the fundamental concept of ecosystem in an obvious way. The bog's vital interdependence of species and physical environment demonstrate how the concept of "organism" can extend to an ecosystem: many parts functioning as a unique whole. Such an object lesson is not trivial, in the face of the challenges we pose to the integrated global ecosphere.

Certainly humans need to use natural resources, just as all other creatures do to one extent or another. We need food and water and oxygen and space for homes and activities. We need to marvel at the beauty of wild creatures. The natural landscape has been a fundamental element in the evolution of human cultures. Many of these values Burns Bog provides. However, its destiny appears to be one of irresponsible abuse, rather than one of sustaining values. This book addresses many of these vital values and contrasts them with increasingly destructive uses.

I had come to British Columbia to learn from human teachers, yet my most important lessons came from the greatest teacher of all, nature itself.

Burns Bog represents the last great tract of a once widespread and globally distinctive ecosystem characteristic of the Fraser delta. It must be preserved.

Richard Joseph Hebda
Victoria, British Columbia

Sunlight and pond lilies on a Burns Bog lagoon.   *Don DeMille photo.*

Chapter One

An Introduction to Burns Bog

*"Burns Bog is a magical place, a resource of immense value,
in terms of both education and recreation."*

David Bellamy
Author, broadcaster and naturalist

After hours of hiking through waist-high tangles of Labrador tea and salal, I'm beginning to appreciate the enormous size of Burns Bog. We enter a stunted forest and my guide, biologist Don DeMille, a tall lanky man with sandy hair and a beard, points to mature pines, the tallest barely two metres high. "Like the bonsai forest?" he grins. I'm more concerned with the ground quivering beneath me like a giant waterbed.

"The lagoons aren't far," DeMille says, striding ahead. Lagoons in a bog? So much has surprised me on this hike that I just shrug and follow him.

Barely out of the magic forest, I stop, stunned by the wild beauty ahead. A series of lagoons blaze yellow with blooming water lilies. Brown and green sphagnum moss carpets the sides of the lagoons. Two hawks shriek overhead as they spiral upward, their broad tails glowing red. The soporific scent of Labrador tea floats in the air.

Before this hike all I'd known about Burns Bog could be summed up in one word—a dump. Like most Lower Mainland residents, I always associated Burns Bog with the Greater Vancouver Regional District's garbage dump. The huge GVRD landfill, south of the City of Vancouver, occupies the southwestern corner of the bog.

Now I realize Burns Bog is hardly a dump—it's a wilderness in the midst of a metropolis, located between the Fraser River and Boundary Bay. A staggering

4,000 hectares, Burns Bog is ten times the size of Vancouver's Stanley Park and is home to 178 bird and mammal species, including threatened sandhill cranes, bears and deer. The bog also boasts rare Mariposa butterflies and plants usually found in alpine areas.

The very nature of the bog—too acid for crops, too wet for cattle and too big to drain—had for centuries defeated every attempt to subdue it. Not any longer. The bog now faces myriad threats: a proposed expansion of the city landfill, increasing private dumps, commercial developments including golf courses, and a highway that could bisect the bog and open it for development.

In 1988 local citizens, helped by eco heavyweight David Suzuki, successfully defeated a $10.5 billion megaport project. The proposal called for a city of 125,000 built around a port complex. Next came an 800 hectare race-track project, also rejected. And now there's a proposal to run a four-lane highway through Burns Bog.

"Care for some tea?" DeMille asks after we photograph the lagoons. Tea in the middle of nowhere? DeMille delights in my astonishment. "Wild bog tea," he says, pulling his thermos from his backpack. Earlier I wondered why he was picking leaves from bushes.

The combination of Labrador tea, salal berries and flowers proves refreshing, with a kick that ad writers might call "the taste of wilderness."

Standing by the lagoons, DeMille explains they're not really lagoons, lakes or even ponds, but deep scars left by peat excavation 25 years ago and now filled with water. DeMille describes Burns Bog as "a garden that gardens itself for nothing."

His love of the bog and his passion in defending it move me. DeMille roamed Burns Bog as a kid and now, as a man, he is defending the playground of his youth, so his children can enjoy it.

After my first hike, I stop at the busy Burns Bog Conservation Society office, located a few miles from the bog. Four staffers check a poster of bog plants, while two students work on a Burns Bog booklet.

President Eliza Olson briefs me on peatlands. I learn that bogs, swamps and some marshes produce peat, which is slowly decaying plant material. Left long enough, peat becomes coal. Peatlands, defined as waterlogged areas with decomposing organic matter, exist around the world on all continents except Antarctica. Everywhere, they're under pressure.

In Russia, Germany and the rest of Europe, peatlands have been exploited as a fuel source. In Ireland only 5 percent of peatlands survive. Controversy over Ireland's famous bogs led to a boycott of peat products in Britain. The European Parliament passed a resolution urging Ireland to protect its bogs.

One name keeps appearing in newspaper clippings and articles in the society's library—Dr. Richard Hebda, who earned his Ph.D. studying Burns Bog. "Wetlands are under severe attack," he confirms when I interview him at the Royal B.C. Museum in Victoria.

Hebda explains the extremely varied ecological functions of wetlands: water purification and storage, flood reduction and control, and wildlife habitat. Bogs also play a vital role in global warming.

"Burns Bog provides one of the very few ways of scrubbing carbon dioxide

Mount Baker broods over the bog. *Don DeMille photo.*

from our atmosphere," he tells me. "Bog plants convert atmospheric carbon dioxide to plant matter which, upon their death, is permanently stored as peat."

Acting as carbon sinks, bogs play a passive but positive role in counteracting global warming. A *sink* is a term used to describe something that absorbs something else. A *source* is the opposite. A living tree is a carbon sink as it absorbs carbon dioxide. A dead tree is a carbon source as it releases carbon dioxide.

"Draining the bog or burying it leads to peat decomposition and release of carbon and methane, a very potent greenhouse gas," he warns.

Burns Bog, as the largest raised peat bog on the west coast of North America, and the largest undeveloped urban land area in Canada, faces enormous pressure. While the preserve or develop controversy rages, the GVRD's landfill continues to receive a quarter of the Lower Mainland's garbage—a whopping 400,000 tonnes a year.

The dump has been described as an eco time bomb, because of the unstable land it sits on. An inner ditch surrounding the landfill is pumped to the Annacis Island sewage treatment plant and contributes 10 percent of the ammonia flowing through the plant. Ammonia is toxic to fish. Numerous private landfills closer to the Fraser River also pose a risk to the 800 million fish migrating to the sea via the broad channel of the Fraser River north of the bog.

The bog swarms with wildlife. There are a dozen bears and 100 deer. Birds of prey include peregrine falcons, gyrfalcons, merlins, kestrels, and a variety of owls as well as bald eagles. The magnificent trumpeter swan and the endangered sandhill crane also inhabit the bog.

In late summer I tag along with a TV crew on a hike into the bog. The cameraman films bird expert Dr. Mary Taitt as she explains that Burns Bog, along with Boundary Bay, is a vital stop for waterfowl on the Pacific Flyway. Each year birds from three continents converge on the bog and surrounding Boundary Bay area. It is considered the best migratory stopover on the coast between California and Alaska.

What lies in the future for Burns Bog? The fundamental question in this preserve or develop dilemma is whether the bog is worth saving. David Suzuki says, "Burns Bog is one of a vanishing kind—a special bit of nature as it has been for millennia. It should be left completely alone." Hebda adds, "You will not find such a large self-contained raised bog with the same species anywhere else in the world. Burns Bog is an exceptional ecological treasure." David

Bellamy says, "Burns Bog is Vancouver's own backyard wilderness, a nature reserve of international importance as well as an enormous carbon sink."

What would be the impact of developing Burns Bog? Locally, Burns Bog helps to maintain air quality by absorbing greenhouse gases, and cools the atmosphere. In 1990 over 600,000 tonnes of pollutants were released into the air, according to the GVRD. Small wonder that on some days Vancouver's smog is worse than Los Angeles'. Functioning as the lungs of the Lower Mainland, Burns Bog directly affects our quality of life.

One warm autumn evening, I join Don DeMille to taste his mother's bog-berry pie and sip homemade bog wine. We celebrate his feat of photographing a dozen sandhill cranes together in the bog. To see so many of these rare, magnificent creatures against the backdrop of the distant city is moving, an image that captures both the mystery and the magic of Burns Bog.

"Got something else to show you," DeMille says. We drive to the bog, park and walk up a path. A bulldozer has torn a wide swath deep into the bog. DeMille says nothing when we reach the end of the ugly track. The shredded bark, mangled trees and shrubs sticking up through the dirt say it all.

While various provincial, federal and international agencies continue to study and survey the bog, development slowly destroys it.

"Each day we do nothing," DeMille says, "an acre of the bog is lost."

Blooming bog laurel.   *Don DeMille photo.*

Chapter Two

How Burns Bog Formed

"An exceptional treasure, the result of thousands of years of development."

Dr. Richard Hebda
Royal B.C. Museum

 One million years ago, ice sheets covered most of Vancouver as they advanced toward the Pacific. The ice mass moved under its own enormous weight, pushing silt, sand and gravel into the sea. During this Ice Age, Vancouver resembled Greenland, with icebergs calving from the ice sheets and drifting out to sea. Inland, lava flowed from volcanic eruptions and mammoths and mastodons roamed North America.

As world temperatures fluctuated, the restless ice sheets responded by advancing or retreating. At times these successive glaciations buried all but the highest of the Coast Mountains, as well as compressing the land under ice 1,500 metres thick.

About 14,000 years ago the climate warmed. The huge dome of ice began to thaw, forming smooth, white glaciers that ground their way to the sea. The glaciers acted like ice rafts, carrying boulders as large as houses. Evidence of rock debris from dying glaciers can be found in marine silts and clays.

The retreating ice left a depression in the Strait of Georgia, allowing salt water from the sea to cover much of the Vancouver area. About 10,000 years ago, the ice finally disappeared from most of southwestern B.C. Freed from the weight of ice, the land slowly rose "to breach the surface of the Strait of Georgia like the back of an enormous whale," according to Dr. Richard Hebda of the Royal B.C. Museum.

About 5,000 years ago, the Strait of Georgia extended east to New Westminster. After the massive meltdown, the Fraser River began to build its delta. Gradually, the sediments it discharged formed deposits of sand, silt and clay many metres thick. This created a new land surface projecting outward in a fan shape toward the Strait of Georgia. The massive volume of sediment continues its seaward expansion to this day, advancing the delta three metres each year near the surface and as much as nine metres below the surface.

Over the course of 5,000 years, Burns Bog evolved from tidal flats to a raised peat bog. Alluvial deposits of sand and silt allowed plants to get a foothold. Soon clumps of rushes and cattails began to grow in the mixture of salt and fresh water. When these plants died, their remains provided a place for new plants to root. What was once a

Rugged shore pine.   *Don DeMille photo.*

brackish marsh was evolving into a wetland with sedges and grasses. Eventually the surface would rise above flood level, allowing shrubs to spread.

About 3,500 years ago another crucial change was taking place. As leaves, stems and roots died, they formed an acidic peat, and this layer of dead plant material slowly elevated the surface. With the bottom consisting of layers of impervious clays, water could not escape easily, creating the cool and acidic conditions that enabled Ice Age plant relics to grow in what became a temperate climate. This combination of rising level and clay bottom slowly shut off much of the bog to the nutrient-rich river water of the Fraser until the bog depended mainly on rainwater.

These acidic and wet conditions suited sphagnum mosses perfectly. They established themselves well and eventually carpeted much of the bog. Mosses, primitive plants lacking a root system, function as sponges, absorbing up to 30 times their weight in water. Mosses absorb moisture from rainwater as well as drawing up water from the peat beneath.

The flora of Burns Bog include many species besides sphagnum moss. Just as a forest is not made of a single type of tree, a bog is not only sphagnum moss. Many different sedges, shrubs and trees as well as numerous plants and flowers thrive in the bog.

Over time, the plants in Burns Bog died, forming layers of peat. The lower material consisted of rushes and sedges, with mosses above. Gradually the dead layers piled up, raising the centre of the bog until it resembled an inverted saucer, with the centre dome standing two stories over the outer edges.

How does a bog differ from a swamp, marsh or fen? All are wetlands, but trees dominate swamps, grasses dominate marshes and sphagnum mosses characterize both bogs and fens. Whereas spring water irrigates a fen, rainwater sprinkles a bog. Bogs, swamps and some marshes produce peat, which is slowly decaying plant material. Left long enough, peat becomes coal.

On a cold December day, I visit Dr. Richard Hebda at the Royal British Columbia Museum in Victoria.

"A unique ecological miracle," Hebda calls Burns Bog, explaining that it was "born of the balance of features of the landscape, water movement and living organisms. The landscape setting provides the opportunity, the plants and animals the raw material and the water, the link or vital nourishing fluid of the system."

"Superorganism" is a term Hebda uses to describe Burns Bog, a living thing which continuously grows outward.

Hebda explains, "Wetlands are critically important to the health of ecosystems and to climate, and provide a way of scrubbing carbon out of the atmosphere and storing it." Bogs act as carbon sinks, absorbing carbon dioxide—the principal cause of global warming—from the atmosphere and storing carbon in the form of peat.

Forestry Canada estimates that about 15 percent of the world's organic carbon is stored in peatlands, while forests hold only 8 percent. If peatlands are disturbed, these greenhouse gases will escape, accelerating global warming. Canada bears a heavy responsibility, as the country holds a quarter of the world's wetland area. Canada's vast wetlands cover 14 percent of the country, more than 90 percent of which are peatlands.

For thousands of years, native people who inhabited the Fraser delta used Burns Bog. In summer, villages were set up in the bog to coincide with salmon runs. When the first white settlers arrived, they diked the lowlands surrounding the bog, then tried draining it without success.

"Human activities such as clearing, burning, draining and filling substantially altered the remarkable self-sustaining biophysical system of the bog," Hebda tells me. "Yet Burns Bog, like an enormous scarred being, survives as the paramount example of a northwest North American raised peatland."

Today Burns Bog remains surprisingly intact, as resilient as the spongy moss that spring back underfoot. But how much longer will this huge chunk of land, situated only a half-hour from the skyscrapers of downtown Vancouver, escape development?

Islets in a bog lagoon.   *Don DeMille photo.*

TIME LOG

1 million years ago	1,500 metres of ice cover the Fraser delta
14,000 years ago	The ice sheet begins to melt
10,000 years ago	Much of southwestern BC rises 150 metres, freed from the weight of the ice sheets
10,000 to 9,000 years ago	The sea extends to the Surrey Uplands, at the base of Panorama Ridge, which rises 80 metres above sea level
9,000 to 7,000 years ago	First native peoples inhabit base of Panorama Ridge
8,000 years ago	An early Fraser delta begins to form from sediment carried toward the Strait of Georgia
5,000 years ago	These sediments continue to build up and plants take hold in brackish marshes
3,500 years ago	Burns Bog rises above tidal levels as peat accumulates. Point Roberts is still an island
Present day	Delta continues advancing westward toward the Strait of Georgia at up to 9 metres a year

Drake mallard over a central bog lagoon.   *Don DeMille photo.*

Chapter Three

Three Diverse Ecosystems — A Bog, a Bay and a River

"If we are indeed to achieve a 'livable region' in Greater Vancouver, some of these areas will serve us better if left undeveloped as open space, recreation areas or conservancies. In my view, such areas are of greater value if the natural systems within them continue to function."

Barry Leach
Waterfowl on a Pacific Estuary

Like some vital piece of an interlocking puzzle, Burns Bog links two diverse aquatic ecosystems: the Fraser River to the north and Boundary Bay to the south. But only a few thousand years ago, Burns Bog did not exist. At that time, the sea extended to the uprising now called Panorama Ridge, which forms the eastern boundary of Burns Bog. Gradually sediment carried by the Fraser River began to form Burns Bog and the delta.

A wide channel of the Fraser River once cut through what is now Burns Bog, flowing south toward Boundary Bay. The channel branched out in a fan shape before reaching the bay. Over time the 500 to 800 metre-wide channel, 18 metres deep, silted in and about 5,000 years ago it eventually dried up. Meanwhile, Burns Bog was evolving from a brackish marsh into a raised peat bog.

While there is no evidence that underground channels of the Fraser River still transport water from the Fraser River south to Boundary Bay, active springs close to the former channels indicate an aquifer.

According to Environment Canada, aquifers are "underground areas of soil or rock where substantial quantities of water are found."

In 1910 Delta Municipality tapped into the springs at the base of the Surrey Uplands. After a pipe system had been installed, pumps lifted the water from the springs to a concrete reservoir built farther up the hillside. Today the remains of the old pumphouse stand idle, along with a giant cistern. But the springs still flow, as they have for at least a century, with enough volume to be heard over the traffic speeding along Hwy 91. Trout and salmon fry are visible in the streams fed from the source, evidence of the water's purity.

Former provincial minister and longtime Delta resident John Savage says, "The water Delta got back around the turn of the century, long before we connected with the GVRD in the 1950s, came through aquifers. The water still does to this day in East Delta, which keeps irrigation ditches flowing. The water would have to come from an aquifer; I don't see any other system that could supply it, because it's not from runoff from the hills. It's a constant supply of water."

More than two-thirds of the world's freshwater supply is found underground. In Canada, more water is underground than on the surface. The water from aquifers appears at the surface as springs and very often groundwater is interconnected with rivers. According to Environment Canada, "a major outwash sand and gravel aquifer occurs in the Fraser River Valley." These porous sands and gravels were left by the retreating ice sheets. At one time 40 percent of the water supplied to Lower Mainland communities south of the Fraser River came from underground sources. In the Fraser Valley, Abbotsford depends on an aquifer as its water source.

The aquifer on the eastern side of Burns Bog raises more questions than it answers. What is its source? More importantly, does it connect with the Fraser River? The existence of aquifers raises concerns about the impact Burns Bog potentially has on the Fraser River. The river is considered endangered and water quality is a major part of the problem.

In the past, a number of proposals have ignored the poorly understood hydrology of Burns Bog and the surrounding area. One GVRD plan wanted to divert sewage water from the Annacis Island plant to parts of Burns Bog for waste treatment.

Recently, the bog has undergone major disruptions in the natural water system. The building of the Alex Fraser Bridge necessitated the construction of Hwy 91 leading to the bridge. The highway cut through the bog, leaving great swaths of dead trees in its wake. The highway itself, various access roads to the highway, ditching and landfill affected water movement. Burns Bog functions as a single unit, a huge, self-sustaining ecosystem. Disrupting or draining part of the bog affects the bog as a whole.

Boundary Bay is a unique and diverse ecosystem rich in nature and a mecca for recreation. Canoeists paddle the meandering Serpentine River flowing into the bay. Horse riders race along the tidal flats as ultralights crisscross the sky like gigantic stiff-winged butterflies. Sailboats ply the sheltered waters and the beaches are crowded with swimmers.

On the western side of Boundary Bay lies Point Roberts. The bottom tip of the peninsula, although surrounded by water on three sides, and physically cut off from the State of Washington, is part of the United States. The 1846 Treaty of Washington ceded this accident of geography to the U.S. because the southern tip of the narrow point dips below the 49th parallel, which separates Canada from the United States. British Captain George Vancouver named the point in honour of his friend Captain Henry Roberts. The point contains a great blue heron colony, the third-largest in the Pacific Northwest, with almost 400 nesting herons.

Five cranes forage within sight of the city.
Don DeMille photo.

*Beaver
lodge in the
shadow
of Tilbury
Cement.*
Don DeMille photo.

The shallow waters of Boundary Bay and the surrounding uplands consist of a wide variety of habitats, both fresh water and salt water. Pods of orcas play off Point Roberts. Harbour seals bob on the surface, then dive to chase herring, which in turn feed on zooplankton. Shorebirds move in flocks as they probe the mud flats for invertebrates. Farther inland, old-field grasslands support the highest average densities of voles in North America. Females can reproduce every month during breeding season and one square metre of grassland can support two voles. The large numbers of Townsend's voles in turn support resident raptor species, including the barn owl and Cooper's hawk, both listed as vulnerable species. Fields also attract swans and geese.

More than 30 years ago, shellfishing along the 40 kilometre shoreline of Boundary Bay supplied over half the oysters harvested in B.C. as well as other shellfish, including shrimp and crabs. In the early 1960s, contaminated water closed the once thriving fishery.

Today pollution is still a major problem.

"Tests for arsenic, cadmium, chromium, lead, mercury, carbon and toxicity all showed higher than average readings for the offshore site in Boundary Bay," states the Boundary Bay Conservation Report.

Water quality is also a problem with the Fraser River running north of Burns Bog. The mighty Fraser and its network of lakes and tributaries drain over 230,000 square kilometres, over a quarter of the land mass of B.C.—an area as large as Great Britain. The Fraser has been described as the main artery of B.C., with two-thirds of the province's population living close to the river or in the Fraser Valley.

The Fraser is a river in crisis as a result of mushrooming urban sprawl. Greater Vancouver is Canada's fastest-growing urban centre, with 2.4 million people concentrated in a small area. Over the next 25 years, the number of people will increase to 3 million, adding to the pressure on the Fraser and the delta's remaining wetlands.

In May of 1995, the B.C. Outdoor Recreation Council named the Fraser "the most endangered river in B.C." In the same month, an advisory management board consisting of representatives from government, native peoples and the general public, issued the critical finding of a two-year study. The board gave the Fraser River basin a failing grade in the area of sewage. Three months later, in August of 1995, the sockeye fishery was closed due to drastic reductions in the size of the Fraser River run.

For 10,000 years this great river has been used by First Nations people. Natives lived off fish from the Fraser. Salmon became the medium of exchange, the "dollar bill" used by coastal natives to barter with tribes of the Interior. With salmon so plentiful, First Nations did not need to grow crops or hunt game. Salmon was more nourishing and had more calories than beef.

The bounty of salmon supported large villages along the Fraser. Explorer Simon Fraser wrote of 1,200 natives greeting him at the mouth of the Stein River.

The arrival of the first settlers transformed the river. As early as 1835, before Fort Victoria was founded, the Hudson Bay Company shipped salted salmon to Hawaii. By 1870 the first cannery opened on the Fraser at Annieville, below New Westminster.

Today, logging operations dump sediment into the river. Pulp mills release toxins and agricultural runoff contributes insecticides and fertilizers. Oil refineries, shipyards, chemical plants, sawmills, landfills and other industrial operations discharge a variety of chemicals ranging from dioxins and furans to heavy metals. Add to this chemical soup two million cubic metres of wastewater pumped daily into the Fraser. Small wonder the future of this great waterway looks doubtful.

While many people blame industry for polluting the river, David Marshall, who wrote *State of the Basin* for the Fraser River Basin Advisory Board, puts the blame on people. On average, each Lower Mainland resident uses about 3.5 bathtubs of water per day. This household wastewater undergoes only primary treatment, which basically filters out over half the solids. The rest is pumped into the Fraser, and over 90 percent of the sewage in the river originates from the GVRD. Secondary treatment, by comparison, would remove 95 percent of solids and treat 85 percent of the toxic discharge.

This pollution directly affects the salmon fishery, which benefits B.C.'s economy.

"The Fraser is the world's greatest salmon river and if we don't make some changes both in lifestyle and in our institutions, we could lose it," warns Ian Waddell, chairman of the Fraser River Basin Advisory Board. David Suzuki sees the fate of the Fraser as a test of our resolve. "The Fraser River is a symbol for ecosystems everywhere. Its fate will tell us whether we can change our attitude and live in harmony with a natural world that supports us."

Salmon Appearance Puzzles Biologist

In 1996, biologist Don DeMille trapped and photographed coho salmon fry in the stream below Watershed Park Reserve in the southeast corner of the bog. This discovery is as exciting as it is perplexing.

Salmon are not supposed to be in the bog. According to a number of environmental consultants, no salmonids can survive in the bog's waterways, due to acidic water. Also, the complex system of man-made ditches use flap valves, which theoretically do not allow in river or sea water but allow water to flow out at low tide.

How did the salmon fry get there? To complete its life cycle a salmon must journey from its freshwater birthplace to the sea and back. The stream where the fry were found does connect with the sea, after being diverted to a ditch flowing to the Oliver pumping station, which discharges into Boundary Bay. Somehow the salmon fry overcame the flap gates and supposedly acidic ditch system.

In an earlier study, conducted in 1994, DeMille found fish at 112 locations in the ditches and sloughs around Burns Bog. Northwestern salamanders and Pacific Coast newts were also found in the fish traps DeMille used.

Following early settlement, dikes were built along the sea and Fraser River. Later, ditches were dug to drain the delta for agriculture. Burns Bog remained relatively undeveloped until the 1940s, when peat harvesting began. Since then, Burns Bog has been ditched so extensively that most streams and waterways no longer flow along their historic routes.

One example is the northeast interception canal, built along the railway line at the base of Panorama Ridge. This canal diverts Cougar Canyon Creek, which once flowed into the bog. Retired fisheries technician Rob Eldridge says coho, chum, steelhead and cutthroat can be found in Cougar Canyon Creek.

What is the long-term implication of salmon within Burns Bog?

Although salmon are protected under the federal Fisheries Act, the issue is clouded by legal technicalities. According to one argument, since the ditches are man-made, fish within them cannot be considered to be there naturally.

The late Bruce Hutchison wrote in his classic book *The Fraser,* "Of all species living in and beside the river, including man, the salmon is in character the bravest; in body, pound for pound, the strongest; in shape and colour the most beautiful; in its scheme of life the noblest; in its instincts the most mysterious."

Blacktail deer on a bog perimeter road.   *Don DeMille photo.*

Chapter Four

Beware of Bears

"Burns Bog is unique regionally, provincially, nationally and perhaps internationally from an ecosystem perspective."

Provincial Ministry of Environment
Lands & Parks report

Where in North America can a person drive from work, change clothes and hunt for bears in the midst of a metropolis? Only in Burns Bog, located a half-hour from the skyscrapers of downtown Vancouver. "I like bear meat, it's better than pork," says Gary Biggar, who has hunted bear in Burns Bog for years. Bearded and burly, Biggar resembles the bears he hunts. We meet at a restaurant early one Sunday morning. "I'll be wearing a grey cowboy hat and black T-shirt," Biggar had told me.

Born near the bog, his family has lived in Delta for generations. As a boy, Biggar roamed the bog, a gigantic natural playground, sometimes encountering bears. One friend was chased around a silo by a two-year-old bear cub in a playful game of tag.

Like his father and his grandfather, Biggar learned to hunt in the bog when he got older. Now in his mid-30s, he earns a living fishing on the Pacific Ocean. Besides hunting in the bog, he also travels north, to remote parts of the province, to hunt elk and moose. Biggar rarely buys meat, supplying the family larder through his hunting. He doesn't think highly of the deer meat he gets from the bog, claiming that it "must be something to do with the water they drink."

Out on the bog in the spring of 1996, Biggar saw tracks of nine bears. He estimates the overall number at no more than a dozen.

Bears used to den in the watershed area of Delta, but building Hwy 91 caused a shift in hibernating, although Biggar says "bears still cross the fence that was built along the highway. That fence won't stop them, they still get out on the highway and cross." A Delta mother noticed a sow with two cubs crossing Hwy 91 in 1996.

Biggar has found signs of more dens being used within the bog today. "I've checked them out and they are being used a little more now but bears have certainly used them before."

Biggar says the bears "move around according to the time of year. They migrate, same as deer. Certain time of year, in fall, there's a couple of high spots in the bog where deer move to."

Bears also use the edges of the bog, getting into cultivated cranberry and blueberry farms, where "they do pretty good damage."

He dispels the myth of cougars stalking the bog. "You'd see evidence. The dirt in the bog's so soft you see bear prints. If there was a cat running around in there, you'd see tracks because cats use dry trails as they're not crazy about water. I've never seen a cat print out there."

A beaver searches for early spring greens.   *Don DeMille photo.*

A coyote hunts in the bog.   *Don DeMille photo.*

Although he's been asked, he hasn't shown anybody where the sow with the torn ear can be found. "The old sow will stay in one certain area, and sometimes a boar comes in when she's with cubs. I've heard the ruckus, when she's chasing him outta her area."

Biggar mainly hunts deer in the bog. The bear is a bonus. A license is needed to hunt bears in the spring. Besides the license, a hunter needs written permission to hunt on the privately held portions of the bog. The permission is a necessity as a full-time caretaker lives in and patrols the bog.

Since he first started roaming the bog as a six-year-old, Biggar has seen a lot of changes. The fringes of the bog are now "industry all around, with farms on the other side." He worries that making the bog an ecological reserve will "mean no one can step foot in it, which wrecks it, if you can't even go out there for a walk to enjoy it." Biggar's facing other changes, especially in the commercial fishing industry where he works. "It's another tradition that's going out."

He also worries about another tradition changing. His son, Gary Jr., 15, might end the Biggar family tradition of hunting in Burns Bog. "If he wants to

1. Flying Squirrel
2. Coyote
3. Blacktail Deer
4. Black Bear & cub
5. Weasel
6. Porcupine
7. Muskrat
8. Pacific Treefrog
9. Garter Snake
10. Beaver
11. Raccoon
12. Red Fox
13. Rabbit

A northwest salamander in the bog.   *Don DeMille photo.*

be a hunter, fine, if he doesn't, well, that's fine also. But he does like eating game meat," Gary Sr. chuckles, "so I guess I'll have to keep supplying him with it."

Due to its size and location, Burns Bog has become a haven for wildlife. As more of the surrounding area is developed, and the edges of Burns Bog are whittled down, the pressure increases. Eleven bird species that use the bog are considered at risk according to the province's Wildlife Species Evaluation list. The blue listing means the species are vulnerable. The bird species on the blue list include: the sandhill crane, great blue heron, bald eagle, gyrfalcon, least sandpiper, California gull, barn owl, ring-billed gull, Vaux's swift, northern shrike and peregrine falcon.

Mammals in the bog include: blacktail deer, raccoons, beavers, muskrats, skunks, porcupines, Douglas squirrels, Pacific water shrews and northwestern jumping mice. Predators include the red fox, coyote and bobcat. Up to 18 species of amphibians and reptiles have been recorded in the Fraser River Valley, but the exact number living within Burns Bog is not known. The more vocal Pacific tree frog, bullfrog and green frog reveal themselves and garter snakes inhabit the bog. Numerous insects also inhabit the bog, including delicate damselflies. The bog also boasts the uncommon Mariposa butterfly.

Wildlife is so plentiful that on one summer hike with botanist-guide Hollis Kelly, the group I accompanied photographed sandhill cranes, a coyote and two redtailed hawks all before the hike officially started. Once into the bog, our group encountered two deer strolling across our path. The deer paused long enough for me to change camera lenses.

With an estimated 100 or so deer in the bog, sightings are frequent throughout the bog. Most of my sightings have been at twilight.

Once my daughter Danielle and I watched a group foraging, backlit by the golden rays of the setting sun. Danielle described it as "a magic moment," sharing this wild garden with its animal inhabitants.

How many major cities can boast of a population of up to a dozen bears living within the metro limits? Only a half-hour away from the hustle and bustle of the steel and glass skyscrapers of downtown Vancouver, bears roam Burns Bog, feasting on the abundance of berries and vegetation. While the novelty of man and bear peacefully coexisting appears attractive, in reality the bears of Burns Bog are now isolated in an ever-shrinking pocket of wilderness surrounded by urban areas.

A weasel in the bog.
Don DeMille photo.

The magic of the crane dance. Don DeMille photo.

Chapter Five

A Vital Stop for Migratory Birds

"Burns Bog is an essential habitat both as a nesting and staging area for Lower Mainland population of greater sandhill cranes. Land owned by Western Delta Land Inc. at Burns Bog comprises the core area of the bog and needs to be acquired or protected in order to ensure long term habitat availability for sandhill cranes."

Gebauer Report
for the B.C. Ministry of Environment

In February, flocks of 10,000 dunlins gracefully weave in tight patterns, streaking the sky white and brown. Below them, 5,000 western sandpipers noisily squeak as they advance up the mud flats of Boundary Bay. A diving dark blur disrupts the nervous feeding of the shorebirds. Instantly they take flight, tumbling in unison to avoid the swoop of the bird of prey. The restless shorebirds twist and turn as the falcon hurtles upward to disappear into the underbelly of gunmetal grey clouds.

Zoologist Dr. Mary Taitt calls the Boundary Bay area "the hot spot in Canada for birds of prey. The density of raptors is phenomenal."

Other resident raptors include redtailed hawks, rough-legged hawks, northern harriers, merlins, kestrels and owls: great-horned, barn and short-eared. Snowy owls and gyrfalcon from the Arctic overwinter here and the area boasts the highest numbers of bald eagles in the Lower Mainland. Biologist Don DeMille has counted more than 200 bald eagles around the landfill in winter.

Each year 1.5 million birds from three continents and 20 countries converge on the Fraser River delta. Burns Bog and the surrounding Boundary Bay area are reputed to be the best migratory stopover on the coast between California

1. Greater Sandhill Crane
2. Canada Geese
3. Black-capped Chickadee
4. Bald Eagle
5. Mallard Ducks
6. Ring-necked Pheasant
7. Great Blue Heron
8. Peregrine Falcon
9. Barn Owl
10. Northern Harrier
11. Trumpeter Swan

2

3

4

and Alaska. In autumn waterfowl of many species, including swans, geese and ducks as well as loons and grebes, converge in great numbers. Close to 140,000 ducks and an equal number of shorebirds rest here at one time. The birds are drawn by the combination of an abundance of food provided by the bay's tidal flats and beds of eelgrass, the protection offered by the bordering farmland at night and the mild winter climate.

Flocks of 100,000 densely-packed western sandpipers sweep across the sand, their underparts flashing white. These "peeps," named for their squeaky calls, are the most numerous species, with the longest migration route stretching from Panama to the Arctic. Half the world's population of western sandpipers stop here each year to feed before flying north to their summer nesting grounds.

Some 50 shorebird species stop along the B.C. coast. Besides being a critical stopover on the Pacific Flyway, the Fraser River estuary boasts the greatest number of overwintering birds in Canada. Even in winter, Burns Bog supports 10,000 waterfowl.

Resident bird species include the great blue heron, often found patiently stalking fish and crabs along Boundary Bay and in marshes and ditches throughout the Fraser delta and in Burns Bog. Herons also forage on grasslands for voles. At night herons fly off to roost in tall trees. The great blue heron rookery in Point Roberts ranks as the third-largest in the Pacific Northwest. The great blue heron has been successfully raising offspring in the delta since the ice sheet melted. Heron remains found in First Nations middens date back 3,500 years.

Despite the need to preserve habitat, a mere one percent of the Fraser River estuary's almost 700 square kilometres is protected under legislation. Because of its importance as an international wetlands site, Burns Bog is under consideration as a "RAMSAR" site. (To achieve this special designation, named after the Iranian town that hosted a seminal wetlands conference in 1971, the area must be considered a vital wetland site of international importance by the United Nations.) Another proposal calls for the entire Boundary Bay area to be declared a UNESCO (United Nations Educational and Scientific and Cultural Organization) Biosphere Reserve to protect its diversity. At present there are 280 biospheres in 71 countries and 6 in Canada. None exists in B.C.

One animal symbolizes the plight of Burns Bog—the greater sandhill crane. These majestic cranes need shallow ponds and open terrain to nest and raise their young. Burns Bog is one of the few remaining areas left in the Fraser delta that can provide both food and protection from predators.

A redtailed hawk on the lookout for lunch.   *Don DeMille photo.*

Once huge flocks of migrating cranes returned each spring to raise their young along the Fraser River Valley. Sandhill cranes occupy a special spot in Katzie legend, where they are regarded as guardian spirits. Now only a few return to Burns Bog, one of the last refuges for cranes in the Fraser delta. The drastic decline in crane numbers prompted the B.C. Ministry of Environment to officially list them as "vulnerable."

Despite its vulnerable status, the greater sandhill crane is a survivor. Carbon dating of fossilized remains tells us the ancestor of today's crane goes back 60 million years to the time of the dinosaur.

Having survived the dinosaurs and the last Ice Age, the sandhill crane now faces the greatest threat to its continued existence—humans. Extensive wetlands along the Fraser River once lured thousands. As the wetlands were diked, drained and developed, the size of the great flocks also shrank, until now only a small remnant migrates to the delta each year. Burns Bog, along with the Pitt River area, is the last refuge for these magnificent birds. Only about 20 to 30 congregate in Burns Bog each fall, which serves as a staging area prior to the flock heading south. The exact numbers nesting in the bog are not known, but surveys show that the cranes are on the borderline of sustainability.

The greater sandhill crane, a subspecies of the sandhill, is tall and stately, with long legs and neck. The greater sandhill stands 1.22 metres tall, with a wingspan between 1.8 and 2.1 metres. Adults are grey with a bald red crown, while the young are brownish. Cranes are omnivorous, with food ranging from frogs to grain.

In flight cranes alternate between gliding and flapping with their neck fully extended. Great blue herons, large birds superficially similar to cranes, fly with their necks folded back.

The call of sandhill cranes is a rolling *garooo-a* audible over a great distance. Cranes lay their spotted olive-coloured eggs on a reedy mound. Both parents share incubation and rear their young.

Both sexes are similar in appearance. In spring, sandhill cranes hop and flap in a spectacular ritual mating dance. Sandhill cranes live up to 20 years and can begin breeding at as early as three years of age. Females lay clutches of two eggs once a year and rarely does more than one chick live to fledge. The cranes stage together in autumn and usually fly south in a V-formation toward the end of October. Although no one has tracked the flight of cranes from the Fraser delta, experts think they fly south to overwinter in California's Central Valley. The flock returns around mid-March to early April.

A recent report by Martin Gebauer for the B.C. Ministry of Environment notes that sandhill cranes need isolated tracts of open bog to nest. The report states, "Cranes also used peat cutting ponds at Burns Bog." The cranes feed on insects, invertebrates and frogs. They also browse in nearby freshly seeded fields and pastures.

Cranes in Burns Bog hunt two types of voles, the western redbacked vole and Townsend's vole, and deer mice. Frog prey includes four species: the red-legged frog, green frog, bullfrog and Pacific tree frog.

When foraging in nearby agricultural fields, the sandhill cranes prefer recently harvested fields or those planted with winter wheat or rye. Flocks of cranes often stage or stop over in harvested fields of corn, wheat or barley before migrating south.

The latest population survey, in 1994, estimated the Fraser delta flock to be 28 cranes. In 1993, no chicks were observed in Burns Bog, but observers the next year spotted three chicks.

Crane sightings in fields west of Burns Bog in the area of Crescent Slough have been consistent over the past two decades. Fall surveys have been conducted fairly regularly, although ongoing studies of cranes have been sporadic. The B.C. Ministry of Environment studied cranes in some depth over the two-year period between 1993 and 1994, with another crane study taking place in

1983. By contrast, the autumn surveys of cranes foraging in open fields started in 1973. The average number of cranes reported over the past 20-year period is 21, with a high count of 33 in one flock in 1991.

Gebauer's report for the B.C. Ministry of the Environment concludes: "The Lower Mainland population of greater sandhill cranes is threatened by habitat loss and alienation, human disturbance and possibly predation. Large tracts of suitable habitat with low disturbance is one of the primary requirements for nesting and roosting sandhill cranes. Important unprotected habitats still exist, especially at Burns Bog."

The report also recommends that the greater sandhill crane's present blue listing as "vulnerable and sensitive" be upgraded to "threatened and endangered," the highest designation in British Columbia, as "it is apparent that current British Columbia populations of cranes are low and may be on the decline."

Trumpeter swans in a bog meadow.   *Don DeMille photo.*

The carnivorous sundew.   *Don DeMille photo.*

Chapter Six

A Refuge for Ice Age Plants

"...a northern island in a southern clime."

Dr. Richard Hebda
Royal B.C. Museum

"We're taking a trip back through time," Hollis Kelly explains as he leads a group through the bog. He points out that many of the plants in the bog are "relics from the Ice Age." Kelly taught science at the same Delta school for 26 years and since 1972 has been taking students on field trips to Burns Bog. Now semi-retired, Kelly is passing on the tradition by instructing Burns Bog Society members on how to conduct student tours.

Journeying into Burns Bog, Kelly teaches us to adjust our gaze. Instead of looking up at mountains capped in white, we learn to look down at detail. Colonies of red-tentacled sundews rise from mats of moss. Their dewy caps sparkle in the sunlight, resembling miniature crowns of silver. These small plants are carnivorous, cleverly trapping, then devouring insects. Kelly explains bog water is so nutrient-poor that sundews adapted to digesting insects to survive.

Kelly points out Labrador tea, used by First Nations to make medicinal tea. The Haida also used it for sore throats and colds and the voyageurs prized it as a restorative drink. Labrador tea grows in drier areas, forming extensive waist-high thickets with a distinctive aroma.

Another unusual mini-shrub is cloudberry, a low-growing relative of the raspberry, with amber fruit, rarely seen in southern B.C. Uncommon blueberry species abound, including bog bilberry and the delicious type (*Vaccinium deliciosus*), a species usually found in sub-alpine areas. Other colourful and

1. Cattail
2. Damselfly
3. Mariposa Copper Butterfly
4. Dragonfly
5. Hardback
6. Bog Laurel
7. Blueberry
8. Yellow Pond Lily
9. Sundew
10. Monarch Butterfly
11. Salal

5

4

6

8

7

unusual plants are ladies' tresses, a small orchid, and yellow pond lily. Nearly 200 plant species flourish in the bog.

Arriving at an open area of bog, Kelly stops to sip brownish water from a lagoon. He explains that the water is safe to drink as the acidity kills bacteria. Despite his reassurance, my skepticism prevents me from tasting the brown water. He smiles and I suspect he has another surprise for the group.

Kelly walks over to a hummock. He picks up and dramatically holds a wet clump of moss. He speculates that sphagnum moss could be the oldest living entity in the world. Theoretically the top of the plant could still be connected to the original stem dating back thousands of years. The present sphagnum exists "by standing on its ancestors."

To many first-time hikers on the outing with Kelly, Burns Bog seems a confusing mix of ponds, forest and heathland, interlaced with ditches. To understand the different habitats of Burns Bog, Kelly asks us to visualize a saucer turned upside down.

The centre portion of Burns Bog resembles the raised part of the saucer. Within this central portion are a number of open ponds, often

Sopping sphagnum, where peat originates.

Bill Burns photo.

called "lagoons," because of the mats of pond lily flowers which blaze a bright yellow in summer. Some ponds are the result of decades of peat excavation; others are natural depressions.

The surrounding vegetation in this portion of the bog is described as either wet or dry sphagnum heathland, depending on the amount of water. Stunted shore pines grow throughout both types of heathland. Dry heathland has distinctive hummocks—small, raised areas. Labrador tea dominates large areas of dry heathland. Other shrubs include bog laurel, blueberry, bog cranberry and bog rosemary.

Wet heathland features sundews, sedges and rushes, as well as many of the plants associated with dry heathland. Ringing this central, open portion are mixed deciduous and coniferous forests. South and north of the central dome lie pine woodlands. The mixed deciduous area features large stands of birch trees, some one metre in diameter with dense, easily-climbed side branches.

The mixed coniferous forest contains western hemlock, Sitka spruce and western red cedar. Some of the trees are more than 500 years old and 2 metres in diameter at the base. A hundred or more bald eagles flock to these cedars at one time. Dense thickets of hardhack fringe the mixed deciduous forests. The transition zone between the rings of forest features large areas of salal and Labrador tea.

Sometimes the various habitats overlap, and "escapee" plants confuse the overall picture. In areas, cultivated east coast cranberries have "escaped" and now grow alongside their native cousins. Domestic blueberry plants have also taken in other areas, dwarfing the smaller native blueberry.

After our exhausting hike, we have to walk past the 18 metre-high landfill to reach our cars parked near the gates leading to the GVRD's landfill. The group's chatter fades to silence as the towering dump seems to cast a dark shadow over the much lower bog. The stench from the dump overpowers the soporific scent of Labrador tea floating from the bog. Kelly attempts to wrap up the tour by explaining that Burns Bog is unique—a refuge left over from the last Ice Age that should be saved. Garbage trucks heading to the dump drown out his words.

Multiple Uses of Peat

Peat is the first stage in the transformation of vegetation to coal. For centuries peat has been used as a fuel in Europe. Pliny the Elder, in the first century A.D., first recorded this practice in northern Europe where Germanic tribes dried peat, then burned it "to cook their food and warm their bodies chilled by the cold north wind."

Today power plants use carbon-rich peat to generate electricity. Russia, with enormous peat resources, harvests some 200 million tons a year, enough to supply over 75 plants. Ireland's peat currently supplies one-fifth of the country's energy needs.

Other peat-fired plants exist in Finland, which, along with Ireland, is recognized as one of the world leaders in peat technology. Recently Finland advised Jamaica on the feasibility of developing its peat resources. Eventually Jamaica's western coast peat deposits could generate 30 percent of the island's electricity. Using European technology, several Third World countries are using satellites to map their peat resources.

In North America only one peat-fuelled power plant, in Maine, presently generates electricity. Other states, like Minnesota, with seven million acres of peat, double the reserves of Ireland, have considered peat plants.

Peat is primarily harvested in North America for the horticultural industry. Both commercial and amateur gardeners find peat extremely useful for many purposes, ranging from potting soil to pots made from peat which are used to plant seedlings in the ground.

Peat has numerous uses in industry, assisting in the production of metals, several acids and chemicals. Russia has pioneered the manufacture of mineral wax from peat. The absorbent properties of peat make it valuable in hygiene products, as degradable bedding and, when raw, for mopping up oil spills.

Fashionable European health spas have promoted the healing properties of hot peat baths since the 19th century. Peat transmits heat differently and thus the human body can tolerate higher temperatures in a peat bath. As a result, rheumatism and arthritis sufferers benefit from increased blood circulation. Other medicinal properties of peat include creams for burns and ulcers.

Canada harvests between 700,000 and 800,000 metric tonnes annually. Most of this peat is slated for the gardening industry. In 1990 total revenues for horticultural peat topped $90 million.

The Unique Flora of Burns Bog

Sundews

Sundews adapted to nitrogen-scarce bog conditions by becoming insect eaters. Long glandular hairs bristle from each leaf and exude a sticky red fluid which attracts, then holds insects. Once an insect is snared, the hairs bend inward to slowly digest the insect's protein. Two types of sundews are found in the bog: long-leaved and round-leaved sundews. Both species infrequently produce drab white flowers. More than 100 species of this family can be found throughout the world.

Labrador Tea

One of the largest members of the heath family, Labrador tea is a shrub with leathery, narrow leaves about 5 cm long. Dark glossy green on top, the leaves' undersides are woolly with rust-coloured hairs. The evergreen leaves, with their downward-rolled edges, are carried alternately on the stems. The pure white flowers are 1 cm across and cluster in groups of 15 to 20. The fragrant aroma of Labrador tea is unmistakable and has been described as soporific, or sleep inducing. First Nations used its leaves to make a vitamin C-rich medicinal tea for sore throats and colds. The voyageurs prized it as a restorative drink. But the leaves should be steeped, not boiled, as they contain an alkaloid that can cause cramps and paralysis. Labrador tea grows in drier areas of Burns Bog, forming extensive waist-high thickets with their distinctive aroma.

Shore Pine

Dwarf pines grow throughout the bog, in places resembling a natural "bonsai forest" due to their size. Considered a weed tree, the hardy and adaptable shore pine is actually a pioneer. The pollen record of many bogs shows this was the first tree to colonize after glaciers retreated. Shore pines grow under harsh and sterile conditions where other trees cannot: in the cracks of rocks, in sand dunes and on high, wind-lashed ridges. Although stunted and often deformed, this tree is a survivor, assisted by its ability to produce seeds within six years. Another survival mechanism is its ability to quickly recolonize after a forest fire, as intense heat opens its cones. The juicy inner bark can be eaten in spring. The shore pine's nuts are also edible.

Yellow Pond Lily

Yellow pond lilies float gracefully on many ponds in Burns Bog. The glossy green leaves are oval or heart-shaped, rising from a thick creeping rootstock growing underwater. The showy bright yellow flowers may bloom all summer. Gasses inside the squat seed pod expand until the seed capsules explode, scattering the seeds in a spray. The ripe seeds can be roasted, ground into flour or popped like popcorn. The huge rootstocks are rooted up by bears and were used by First Nations as a starchy vegetable.

Cloudberry

Cloudberry is a low-growing relative of the raspberry with yellow coloured berries. This dwarf perennial has a creeping rootstock and upright branches up to 25 cm long. The lobed leaves are round and heart-shaped. A solitary showy white flower rises on an erect stem. The sweet fruit is very juicy, turning yellow and resembling clusters of miniature yellow apples. The plant is another leftover from the Ice Age and the bog represents its southernmost limit. First Nations people picked the berries, considered by many as the most delicious of northern berries.

Crowberry

Crowberry is a very low, matted evergreen plant that creeps along the ground. Its narrow green needle-like leaves resemble tiny fat fir needles. The solitary flowers are small and drab purple. The crow-black berries give the plant its name. The juicy berries have a mild medicinal flavour, with bitter seeds, and can be eaten raw, stored or improved by freezing. In the Arctic, where they are abundant, crowberry is considered the most important fruit of the region. Crowberry is a "far north" plant, ordinarily found in the Arctic and on Interior mountains. It is unusual at such low coastal elevations.

Blueberry

World-wide, there are about 200 species of blueberries. About 25 grow in North America. B.C. boasts some 15 species and a number of them can be found in Burns Bog, including escapees from nearby cultivated blueberry farms. All are

members of the same genus, *Vaccinium,* and members of the heath family. One uncommon blueberry is the delicious type (*Vaccinium deliciosus*), a sub-alpine species usually found only on mountains. Another species ordinarily not found this far south is the velvet-leafed blueberry (*Vaccinium myrtilloides*). All the species, while varying in size, have small and glossy alternate leaves with no prickles. The alternate leaves are deciduous, except on a couple of coastal species. All produce succulent, many-seeded berries.

Cotton Grass

Viewing a field of fluffy cotton grass is one of the delights of visiting Burns Bog. Despite its name, this plant is not a grass but a sedge. A sedge is grasslike, with a single stalk rising from a tuft of narrow leaves. The cluster of small, inconspicuous flowers resembling balls of cotton account for the name. In summer the cottony bristles lengthen to 3 to 4 cm.

Bog Laurel

This beautiful small shrub is a true bog plant similar to Labrador tea. The low evergreen shrub has smooth and slender branches. Its narrow dark green leaves have rolled edges and are glossy above and waxy white underneath. The bog laurel's sculptured buds and elegant rose-pink flowers make it stand out—

even though the small flowers are only 12 mm across. The saucer-shaped flower's pollen-bearing stamens spring outward when an insect touches the centre of the flower. Many regard it as the most beautiful flower in Burns Bog. The leaves and flowers contain a compound which is poisonous to cattle and sheep.

Sphagnum Moss

Sphagnum is the name given to a large family of mosses. In its natural state, sphagnum thrives in wetlands around the world, especially in bogs. Sphagnum is a primitive plant with a stem but without a root. A spore case grows from the leafy stalk, releasing spores when ripe. Sphagnum has been called the zombie plant as it normally grows in huge mats with only its top layer alive, the lower part dead but not decaying. Some species, like *Sphagnum fallax* and *Sphagnum cuspidatum,* prefer deep water and possess long soft leaves. Others, like *Sphagnum fuscum,* are more terrestrial. This species is brown and grows in compact hummocks. *Sphagnum rubellum* is another small species, similar to *Sphagnum fuscum,* except it is red in colour. Sphagnum has two unique properties: one is its exceptional ability to draw up water. This is due to its large and hollow sieve-like cells, which enable it to transport water upward from the water table. This capability of sphagnum to maintain the wet conditions essential for its continual growth allows sphagnum to rise above flat land to form raised or domed peat bogs. Another property of sphagnum is its ability to make ground water acid. As the plant forms moss carpets, the decomposing sphagnum layers underneath ooze acid and eventually the nutrient-poor and acid water make the bog fit only for sphagnum and similar plants. Thus it eliminates competition by poisoning the water.

Fire in the bog.   *Courtesy Rick Loughran, Vancouver Province.*

Chapter Seven

Fire in the Bog

"The lungs of the Lower Mainland are smoking."
Biologist Don DeMille

 Tuesday, July 16, 1996, begins as another hot summer day in the Lower Mainland. A little past noon, a Delta firefighter, travelling on Hwy 91 next to Burns Bog, notices smoke rising from the bog. Once the alarm is raised, Delta firefighters respond quickly. Within a half-hour, a crew locates the fire about two kilometres inside the bog from Hwy 91 and 72 Avenue. Whipped by a rising wind, the fire quickly spreads through the dry bush, until it is tree-topping. The fire crew, driven back by the out-of-control blaze, calls for help from the forest service.

Within an hour, the first of a number of Abbotsford-based waterbombers roars overhead. The twin-engined Firecat dumps its load but the 3,000 litres of chemical fire retardant have little effect on the rapidly spreading blaze, which now covers more than 20 hectares. Forestry fire officials deploy other waterbombers to combat the fire.

Hours later, a total of nine aircraft and one helicopter crisscross the site. Two surveillance aircraft co-ordinate the aerial fleet consisting of a DC-6 air tanker, six smaller Firecat waterbombers and a helicopter. The giant plume of thick smoke limits visibility and BC Hydro towers make conditions difficult for the aircraft called in to control the blaze. They encircle the outer fringes of the fire, swooping in low, just above tree level, to drop chemical fire retardant in an effort to contain the blaze.

By late afternoon, the raging fire covers 170 hectares. The huge pall of smoke from the fire rises a kilometre into the air. Pushed by a southeast wind, the column of smoke and ash drifts across Richmond and Vancouver, obscuring Vancouver's North Shore mountains. The darkened sky snarls traffic.

Health officials caution people with breathing disorders to stay inside, particularly asthmatics as the smoke could trigger asthma attacks. Aircraft approaching Delta airport are diverted. As the fire rages out of control, Delta police close River Road north of the bog and advise businesses located in the industrial area to evacuate.

As the fire races through the bog, firefighters grow concerned over two BC Gas lines running through the bog. At one point the fire comes within 300 metres of the lines buried 2 metres underground.

After dropping more than 80 loads, the waterbombers' containment strategy begins to pay off. The largest waterbomber, a four-engined DC-6, can drop 10,000 litres in one pass. Two forestry service fire crews join the hard-pressed Delta firefighters in battling the blaze. The three crews tackle the fire at different points, laying hoses to ponds and opening floodgates from the Fraser River to flood portions of the bog.

The fire crews work through the night, despite the danger of sinkholes, soft portions of the bog which can trap a person. A steady rain on Wednesday helps

A helicopter dumps another load of fire retardant.   *Don DeMille photo.*

The fire line. *Don DeMille photo.*

dampen the blaze. Calm wind conditions aid the crews, in contrast to the 11-knot wind that fanned the fire through treetops the day before. Without any fire hydrants, the crews struggle to lay miles of hose. Slowly they establish a perimeter. "We're trying to tighten the ring and work our way toward the centre," explains Delta fire chief Randy Wolsey.

Battling a bog fire can be dangerous. Another Delta fire crew, fighting a bog fire in 1990, became trapped when the wind shifted. Their only escape route was a sawdust-waste road. But the intense heat locked their truck's brakes. The fire raced nearer and the thick smoke made breathing difficult. With their air packs almost out, another firefighter used an all-terrain vehicle to rescue them.

Another fire on the west side of Burns Bog in July 1992 came within 100 metres of an explosives storage area at the end of 60th Avenue. The fire raced down a sawdust road scorching power poles. BC Environmental Hazardous Waste specialists were called in as the blaze headed toward the chemical residue road near the explosives sheds. A major evacuation might have been required had the two helicopters and 16 firefighters been unable to control the blaze.

Three days after the 1996 wildfire erupts, the Delta firefighters are still hosing down hot spots, assisted by 20 forest service firefighters.

"Peat is very porous and there is air in the soil itself. It smoulders and finds its own trails within the peat and travels. It'll pop up just 15 metres from where you're working," says Randy Wolsey.

The smouldering spots prove difficult to stamp out so the firefighters work graveyard shifts all the next week. "We have hot spots coming up all the time," says Delta deputy fire chief Allan Rusk. He explains how the wildfire continued to burn a metre below the surface in some areas. "It takes lots of men and lots of time," adds Rusk.

Finally, the firefighters reach the centre of the fire. The charred wasteland, with blackened trees, twisted roots and ditches, presents problems due to its remoteness and rugged terrain. The fire crews use a special compound, which soaks quickly into the peat. After hosing the foamy liquid onto the peat, the crews follow up by turning over the peat by hand to make sure the fire can't spread underground.

While fire crews struggle to extinguish the underground fire, Delta fire-fighters and police investigate the cause of the wildfire. "We're satisfied that the fire was started accidentally," Constable John Horsfall says, explaining that two men went to the fire department after the blaze erupted and admitted they dropped a cigarette in the bog during the afternoon of July 15. "They saw they started a fire and doused it with water. They thought they put it out. Obviously they didn't, because 24 hours later it broke out again."

Horsfall confirms that the investigation traced the movements of the two men along an access road to the west of Hwy 91 in the bog. They conclude the blaze started near the spot where the men accidentally discarded a cigarette. No charges will be laid.

P. W. Steblin, Delta's director of engineering, says, "It is anticipated that the area will recover quickly. There were a number of pockets of unburned areas over much of the area, which should aid in the bog's recovery. Fire is a natural process and some plants actually require fire to complete their cycle. Ecologically there will be some short-term scarring, but over the long term there will probably be a net benefit to the area."

Burns Bog, as a domed peat bog, is dependent on rainwater. Hot summer conditions dry out portions of the bog, making the bog vulnerable to fire. Peat, one stage away from coal, is still used as fuel in parts of Ireland. Fires have traditionally occurred during dry summers. An especially stubborn blaze burned for weeks in the summer in 1977. The following summer, Delta fire chief J. Tapio recommended closure of Burns Bog due to the fire hazard and lack of access for fire equipment. Council ordered the bog closed to public access until September 30, 1978. Other fires broke out in Burns Bog in 1990, 1992 and again in 1994.

"Fire has been a profound shaper of the bog," says biologist Don DeMille as we trudge through the scarred terrain a month after the blaze erupted. Our footsteps stir up clouds of ash so thick DeMille asks me to walk beside him to stop the ash from making his eyes water.

The surrounding charred landscape looks surreal, like some mad painter had dumped a layer of grey-black ink over everything. Skeletons of trees, their bare limbs stretching outward, stand silently. At their base, the exposed roots resemble gnarled arms grotesquely twisted in agony. What look like thousands of tiny white buttons are scattered everywhere, contrasting with the blackness. It's almost impossible to take a step without seeing these snail shells, their colouring baked off, exposing the white calcium.

As we continue on our hike, DeMille explains, "Fire is an absolutely natural occurrence and probably is essential to the maintenance of the bog the way it is. Without fire, Burns Bog would have been much different. There are many

Bracken sprouting through the ashes.   Don DeMille photo.

layers of ash as you go down through the layers of peat. This is not a catastrophe, it's part of the natural order of things. Fire will create something temporarily different than what was on this particular site before.

"Many of the plants here are in the heath family, like Labrador tea, so you could see more of an open meadow situation develop here and less of a forest. What may happen is that sphagnum moss may come back to be even more dominant than before."

Ahead, curled heads of bracken break through the sooty surface. Some are almost a metre high, their spreading fronds providing a lacy green relief from the bare blackness. Nearby stands a clump of pine trees. High up, cones are open, seeds ready to recolonize.

DeMille stops to photograph a hummock. "Some of the moss in these hummocks is still living because they held a little more moisture than the surrounding land and were resistant to burning. These little islands will be important as seed distribution centres."

We walk through kilometres of burnt bog, our faces becoming inky with soot. Ever the optimist, DeMille points out that the ash "is incredibly good fertilizer. It will also alter the pH and create conditions that will allow a lot of plants here next spring that wouldn't normally grow in the bog—fireweed, grasses, liverworts and probably a whole lot of hair moss. Ultimately the bog will go back to what it was before."

Halfway through our long trek, we come across part of the old peat railway line. The twisted ties resemble charred ribs. The intense heat from the fire popped many of the 16-centimetre-long spikes. As Don straps himself into a tree to photograph the scene, I begin to appreciate the difficulties the firefighters encountered. In places my feet sink through the ashy surface to the moist peat beneath. By a nearby wide ditch, I almost stumble through the thin surface crust to the dens beavers dug in the bank.

Later we pass an area partly harvested for peat in the 1940s. DeMille explains, "Fire used to be a shaper of the bog but it's not anymore because we put it out. The river above and the sea below were shapers of the bog, particularly the edges of the bog. Now we've diked those off and so now a lot of the natural influences aren't here anymore. So maybe peat harvesting is beneficial because it's created some of the depressions that fires used to create to allow different sorts of plants to get in to support some of the wildlife. For example, the sandhill cranes may have only frequented the parts of the bog that used to burn and regrow afterwards. But without disruption of some sort, either fire or peat harvesting, Burns Bog won't be able to support what it's traditionally supported, if we let it all grow to this dense forest."

Our long hike isn't all serious. DeMille entertains me with his collection of jokes about the fire. He opens with, "The lungs of Lower Mainland are smoking," and ends with a more philosophical and personal comment. "Maybe it's poetic justice that smoke from Burns Bog headed to Vancouver, because for years Burns Bog sucked smoke from Vancouver. Now the bog's giving it back."

At twilight, my knees aching after our exhausting eight-hour hike, we follow bear tracks through a mushy part of the bog. I'm apprehensive and remark that I'm too tired to run if we encounter a bear. DeMille says he's never met one out here. He pauses to photograph a blueberry bush with contrasting blue and delicately tinted pink berries. When we look up, a cream-coloured coyote is only 20 metres away and closing. We watch as the wild animal circles us clockwise, using bushes in the field as cover. Finally Caesar, DeMille's large black lab, sees the coyote and gives chase. Not a good idea.

DeMille shouts and Caesar returns, tail wagging. DeMille is excited, he's never seen such a bold coyote. Suddenly the coyote appears again, circling back, this time counterclockwise. We spot a flash of something light-coloured in the opposite direction. Another coyote, similar-looking, watches us. DeMille's out of film so we stand silently—two men, one dog and two coyotes enjoying the twilight bathing this unique wilderness sanctuary in golden light.

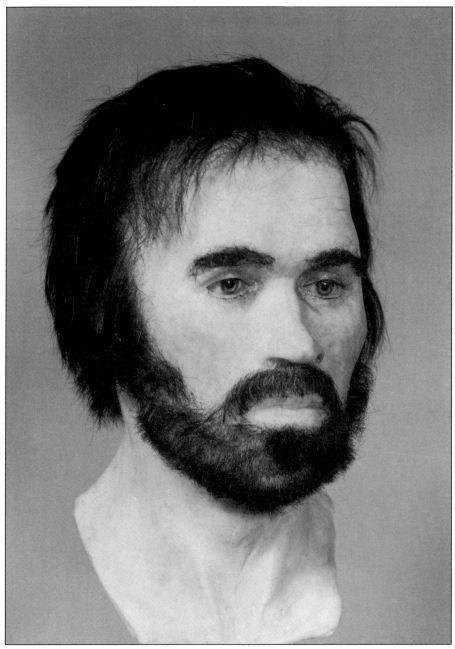

An artist's reconstruction of Lindow Man.   *Copyright the British Museum.*

Chapter Eight

Myth and Mysteries of the Bog

"The peat is the dark casket, where we have found many of the clues to our past and our cultural identity."

Irish poet Seamus Heaney

Throughout history bogs have mystified humankind. The very characteristics that make a bog a bog—the ground quaking underfoot, peat fires, the wet and dank conditions—add to the mystique of these forbidding places. The word *bog* can be traced back to the Celts, an early Indo-European people distributed from the British Isles to Asia Minor. In their language, bog meant "something soft that sinks." *Webster's Dictionary* defines bog as "wet spongy ground."

The Celts regarded bogs as sacred places and practised ritual sacrifice, both animal and human, in bogs. In A.D. 98 the Roman writer Tacitus recorded that Gallic tribes sacrificed humans in bogs. "Cowards, those afraid of war and those guilty of unnatural vice, they deposit in filthy swamps."

In 1984, workers excavating peat in Lindow Moss, outside Manchester in England, found a round clump on a conveyer used to handle sliced peat. One man kicked the object in an impromptu game of soccer. Then he realized it was a human head. Baffled police called in archaeologists, who determined the body was not a recent murder victim, but was, in fact, more than 2,200 years old. The woman's head became known as Lindow Woman.

The horrific discovery led archaeologists to hunt for the rest of the body. Instead, they unearthed the well-preserved body of a man sliced in two. Lindow Man is the most recent and famous ancient body recovered from a bog. Other victims, including Grauballe Man and Tollund Man, were found in Denmark in the 1950s. Both died more than 2,000 years ago. To date, more than 2,000 bog bodies have been discovered in Europe.

Scientists investigating Lindow Man found this Celt had been garroted, his throat slit, his skull smashed and his vertebrae severed in ritual death. Archaeologists speculate that Lindow Man was a Druid priest who voluntarily sacrificed his life to atone for the Roman invasion. The heroic nobleman's death by stabbing, hanging and drowning reflected the Celts' tradition of doing everything in threes, their sacred number as three gods dominated Celtic mythology.

The Roman conquest of Britain provides a motive for the sacrifice of Lindow Man. A new Roman governor, Suetonius Paulinus, attacked the Druids' sanctuary, butchering the priests and destroying their sacred groves. As the Roman governor savoured his victory, he learned of an uprising. Queen Boudicca, who had been flogged by the Romans and whose daughters had been raped, led the revolt.

Swearing vengeance, Boudicca's forces destroyed the Roman city of Colchester. Other tribes joined her uprising and the large force headed toward Roman London. Governor Suetonius sped toward London with his cavalry, ordering his dispersed forces, including the Ninth Legion, to London. Boudicca ambushed the Ninth, completely destroying the Roman force.

The Roman governor, still awaiting reinforcements, abandoned London. Boudicca's forces sacked the city, burning it before turning on a third Roman city, St. Albans. The remaining two Roman legions joined up to stop the Britons. Although outnumbered eight to one, Suetonius' trained legions routed the undisciplined Celts, killing 80,000.

The Roman victory signalled the second of three disasters. First was the destruction of the Druidic sanctuary. The defeat and suicide of Queen Boudicca was the second. Celtic farmers abandoned their spring planting when the Romans began a reign of terror. Famine spread over the country. To appease the gods for the triple devastation, scientists speculate, Lindow Man offered himself to the vengeful gods.

How are bodies preserved in bogs? Under ordinary circumstances bodies decay, and the possibility of human soft tissue surviving for years is so remote it seems impossible. But woolly mammoths have been found frozen in Siberia, so completely preserved that the contents of their stomachs can be identified.

Submerging a body in a bog is an effective way to preserve flesh. This halts nature's usual cycle of growth, death, decay and rebirth at the decay stage.

Saturated in acidic water, oxygen is excluded. This prevents oxidation and bacteria from ravaging flesh. Another unusual characteristic of peat helps preserve flesh. Chemicals in peat convert flesh into a type of leather. While internal organs and bones often dissolve, the acidic stew preserves the outer skin.

As layers of peat accumulate, their weight eventually compresses the body into a boneless leather sack.

Irish bogs have yielded remarkable finds, ranging from extinct animals to objects of gold and bronze. Even butter has been found preserved in peat. The Irish in prehistoric times raised cattle and to conserve the once-a-year supply of spring-calving milk, this was churned into butter and stored in wooden

Lindow Man as he was discovered.   *Copyright the British Museum.*

containers. These were buried in the bog to prevent the butter going rancid. Sometimes these "butter sites" were poorly marked and centuries later unearthed by the blade of a turf cutter. These fascinating subterranean secrets prompted Seamus Heaney to write "Bogland."

Heaney, who won the Nobel Prize in literature in 1995, often connects his writing to the backbreaking labour done by his father and grandfather in digging peat. Heaney says the Irish "bog is a memory bank," preserving everything.

> *They've taken the skeleton*
> *Of the Great Irish Elk*
> *Out of the peat, set it up*
> *An astounding crate full of air*
>
> *Butter sunk under*
> *More than a hundred years*
> *Was recovered salty and white*
> *The ground itself is kind, black butter*

An excerpt from "Bogland"
by Seamus Heaney

Bogs are still considered evil places—dark and decaying. And bogs still provide horrific finds. In 1979 nine skeletons were excavated from a northeast Asian bog. Dr. Alexander Avdonin, who made the discovery, speculated the remains were those of Czar Nicholas II and his family. If he was correct, his find would solve one of the most puzzling mass murders of this century.

On the night of July 16, 1918, the Czar and his family were lined up in two rows in a basement in Ekaterinburg. The Romanovs sat patiently, expecting their photograph to be taken. Instead, a Bolshevik death squad burst into the small room and opened fire.

For the next three-quarters of a century, the riddle of the missing bodies perplexed historians. To compound the mystery, a number of women claimed to be Anastasia, the youngest daughter of the Czar. Researchers tracked down one of the members of the death squad. According to the ghoulish account, the bloated remains were hauled from a mine shaft where they were initially dumped, and piled into a truck. When the truck became mired in a bog, the bodies were covered with lime and buried in the bog.

Could the remains Dr. Avdonin found be the missing Romanovs? The skeletal remains fit the physical descriptions of the Czar and his family. DNA samples taken from the remains matched those of the British Royal Family. Czar Nicholas' wife, Alexandra, was Queen Victoria's daughter. The British monarch, the "grandmother of Europe's royal families," passed her DNA to her daughter, who in turn passed her DNA to her children.

Only one mystery remains—Anastasia's remains were not found in the bog.

Bogs still do not respect leaders, as shown by former U.S. president George Bush's near-fatal encounter with a bog in Newfoundland in July of 1995. While on a fishing trip to Canada's easternmost province, Bush went for a walk. Ground fog obscured his vision and he stumbled into a bog hole and nearly drowned.

"He was in a very serious situation," explained Craig Dobbin, Bush's host. "It was a matter of seconds before he was in over his head." After 10 minutes of struggling, RCMP and U.S. secret service agents freed Bush.

In central Florida, a construction crew unearthed a human skull while working on a housing project. Florida State archaeologists were called in and began excavating the bog. After digging through more than 2 metres of peat, they uncovered remains of native Americans dating back more than 7,000 years. Further digging uncovered a hundred more remains.

One skull contained a surprising find—a shrunken brain. The brain of the native Indian was so well preserved microbiologists were able to extract DNA. This provided a fascinating genetic time capsule—the oldest known human DNA. Scientists are attempting to clone the DNA material to learn more about early native Americans.

Called nature's compost, peat consists of partially decomposed plant remains. Peatlands form natural archives for both plant and, occasionally, animal remains. While bones of vertebrates are rarely found, plant finds are common.

Plants contain virtually indestructible grains of pollen. Peat acts like blotting paper in its ability to hold these small grains from the past. Scientists take peat samples, then carefully examine them for plant remains, microscopic pollen and any insects and bones preserved in them. These vertical columns cut through the peat layers represent "slices of time." Sometimes this leads to exciting discoveries when the remains of extinct plants are found deep within a bog.

By analyzing the preserved vegetation and trapped pollen grains, paleo-botanists can identify past plant communities. The age of the older communities can be established by radio-carbon dating. After studying these samples, a picture of an ancient landscape emerges, showing what plants thrived at what time, as well as providing a look back at how the bog formed and how major natural events affected the environment.

Thus scientists can reconstruct what the world was like thousands of years ago. This reveals what the climate was like—whether temperatures were abnormally higher or rainfall lower. By investigating this paleoenvironmental record of past cycles, scientists are better able to understand not only how peatlands evolved but also how to extrapolate future trends. The historical record of past climate change could resolve the controversy over whether our present period of global warming is a natural cycle or an unnatural phenomenon.

Scientists speculate this will help in predicting future climate change and help solve the world's most pressing ecological problem—how to control global warming.

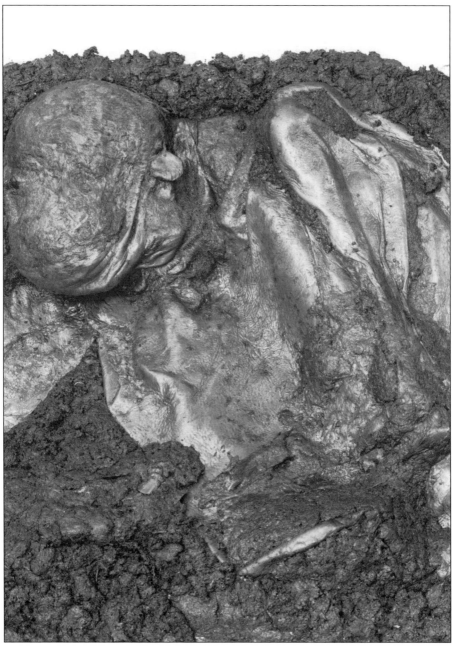

Lindow Man.

Copyright the British Museum.

Cutting peat by hand circa 1940.

Chapter Nine

Heritage and Native Myths of Burns Bog

> *"Cranes are the magic of nature, their voices penetrate the atmos-*
> *phere of the world's wilderness areas ... their footprints have been*
> *left on wetlands of the world for the past 60 million years or more.*
> *They have served as models for human tribal dances ... and their*
> *sagacity and complex social behaviour have provided the basis for*
> *folklore and myths."*
>
> **Paul A. Johnsgard**
> *The Crane Dance*

So many cranes once migrated to the Fraser delta each spring, Katzie First Nations elders said the skies darkened with their arrival. The month of March was the "month of cranes" to these native people living on the lower Fraser River. Now only a few cranes migrate each March. They come to the shallow ponds and open terrain of Burns Bog, which provides both food and protection from predators. The bog is one of the last refuges for cranes in the Fraser delta.

The Katzie held the greater sandhill cranes in great awe, regarding the large birds as guardian spirits. Cranes were especially significant to women, as the crane spirit helped women with their work. One legend tells about Kaahls, a Katzie spirit who watched two sisters gathering food along the river. Instead of digging, the women laughed and mocked Kaahls by dancing. Angered by their display, Kaahls punished the two sisters by transforming them into cranes. Forever after, the two sisters roamed the marshes, cackling and dancing.

First Nations people have inhabited the Fraser delta for an estimated 9,000 years. The Fraser estuary was dominated by the Sto:lo or People of the River. The Sto:lo territory extended up the Fraser River to Yale. Although this First Nations people spoke a similar language, dialects differed from upper river to lower river communities. They used the broad Fraser as their means of transportation. The peaceful and hospitable Sto:lo did not own land: they shared the land and the bounty it provided, although visiting groups would ask permission if the land was traditional territory of another family.

An Indian fishing village.   *Courtesy Delta Archives.*

Tsawwassen Indian Legend

The Tsawwassen band believed an underground channel flowed from the Strait of Georgia into the heart of the bog, where fierce monsters lived. The Tsawwassen band has a myth about a mysterious pole that would appear underwater off Point Roberts. Anyone who held on to the pole would obtain power. Two men dived into the water and swam for the pole but instead fell unconscious under the water. They awoke far from the sea.

The two friends figured there must be some connection between the mysterious power of the pole and the secret stream running into Burns Bog. They went into the bog, lured by the cranberries that got bigger the farther they went in. But one of them fell into a slough guarded by fierce creatures. The other man jumped for a tree while his friend slid farther and was eaten by the creatures. After the creatures had eaten their fill, the surviving native fled.

Swamps covered much of the Fraser delta. In the summer Sto:lo set up temporary villages in Burns Bog to coincide with salmon runs. These runs were so thick the Sto:lo talked of "walking on the backs of fish." At this climactic event of the year, the first salmon caught was ceremonially cooked, then cut into pieces small enough so that there was one for every member of the community.

Burns Bog was a valuable resource, rich in fish, waterfowl, plants and berries. Sphagnum moss, a naturally absorbent material when dry, proved useful for diapers and bandages. Cranberries, blueberries and salal berries were eaten fresh or preserved in cold moss. Labrador tea and other herbs were used as medicinal drinks.

Archaeologists studying the ancient Sto:lo village of Aselaw, also known as Milliken site, a few kilometres north of Yale, date the middens at about 10,000 years, confirming a native presence along the Fraser since the end of the ice age. Another of British Columbia's archaeological sites is located under the Alex Fraser Bridge in North Delta, to the northeast of Burns Bog. Called "Glenrose," after the Glenrose cannery, the site lies on the south bank of the Fraser River. Another important site is St. Mungo's, 1,000 metres downstream from Glenrose. Before the delta grew from sediments carried by the Fraser, this location was the mouth of the Fraser River.

He reached home and realized he had been given secret power. He used this power to successfully fish and hunt. He never used net nor snare, yet all his game, fish, deer and birds, showed blood around the mouth. When children disappeared, then turned up dead with blood around their mouths, the people became angry.

They hunted this secretive young man who had abused his power and killed him. His body was put in a canoe and buried.

This "myth" might be based on fact as it is believed that underground water channels once ran through Burns Bog. Given the underground waterways, a body lost at sea or on the Fraser could resurface in the bog. Such a mystifying occurrence could lead to the "creation" of native myths about bodies appearing in the bog.

The oldest of the artifacts recovered from the Glenrose site in North Delta is estimated to be 4,500 years old, predating the height of the Egyptian empire. Historian Darren Anderson claims that "it's probably the most significant archaeological 'wet' site in North America." Despite the historic value of the excavation, it faces paving as it lies in the path of a proposed highway.

Another site being investigated lies at the southeast corner of the bog, where the Burlington Railway and Hwy 99 meet. Called Under Water by the Sto:lo elders, the site differs from the numerous summer sites used by the First Nations along the Fraser River as this was a permanent village.

A preliminary survey of potential First Nations archaeological deposits in the Fraser delta has identified hundreds of other sites. Unfortunately, many are threatened by development. In 1996 an exhibit of artifacts, "From Under The Delta," was held at the University of British Columbia's Museum of Anthropology, in collaboration with the Musqueam First Nation. A wall panel at the archaeological exhibit states: "Unlike stone monuments in other parts of the world, much of this heritage remains invisible, buried in the wet mud of the river banks and beneath the flat farmlands of the valley and delta. Urban, recreational and industrial growth is destroying this vulnerable hidden dimension of First Nations' history."

The Burns Family

In the mid-1840s, a blight devastated Ireland's "bread and butter" potato crop, leading to widespread starvation. To escape the famine, Michael O'Byrne and Bridget Gibson O'Byrne of County Mayo left the Emerald Isle for Canada in 1848.

The O'Byrnes settled in Oshawa, Ontario, where their first four children were born. Pat, later to become Senator Pat Burns, was born in 1855, and Dominic in 1859. In 1864 the family drove a team of 10 oxen to Kirkfield, where they built a 9 by 7 metre log house chinked with clay and roofed with poles and thatching grass. Their 40 hectare farm overlooked the Talbot River.

The family grew and eventually numbered 11 children. Seven were boys. Along the way, the family name changed to Byrne and then to Burns.

In the early 1880s Pat headed west. He arrived in Manitoba barely a decade after Canada bought the land from the Hudson Bay Company.

The Burns
brothers,
Dominic (left)
and Pat.

Later Dominic followed his older brother west. This was the age of wild expansion of railways, and their childhood friend from Kirkfield, Willie Mackenzie, later to become Sir William, was involved in railway construction. Pat Burns supplied the railway crews with beef. This provided the Burns brothers with their start in the livestock trade.

Pat moved west with the railway, eventually settling in Calgary and continuing to prosper as Canada's "cattle king." His beef trade expanded west and then north, following the Klondike gold rush.

Dominic played a big part, in 1899 leading a mid-winter cattle drive over the White Pass to Atlin after reports of a famine in the new gold rush community. Despite the brutal conditions—deep snow and temperatures of 50°C below zero—Dominic succeeded in delivering the cattle to Atlin. Grant MacEwan, former governor-general of Alberta, described these winter cattle drives of the late 1890s as "undertakings deserving to be listed among the most courageous in agricultural history."

Dominic opened a butcher store in Atlin after arriving with the herd. The beef proved tough but welcome eating. For the next few years Dominic managed the Burns' Yukon beef trade. He remained in the north, as there was money to be made, with beef selling for a dollar a pound. He set up outlets in White Horse and Dawson and opened an office at Bennett. Dominic travelled to Seattle and Oregon to purchase cattle to supply his stores.

Dominic came to Vancouver around the turn of the century and ran the new Vancouver meat plant, built in 1907. The plant not only supplied the various

Burns butcher stores but also shipped meat overseas to the Orient. In 1905 he purchased most of the huge Delta bog that later became known as the Burns Ranch for $26,000.

After assisting his brother Pat for years, he struck out on his own. In 1910 he started construction of the Vancouver Block office building on the highest point of land in downtown Vancouver. When it opened in 1912, the 76 metre building was the tallest in the city. He lived in the penthouse apartment on the 15th floor, under the 12.2 metre clock tower. The 6.7 metre-diameter clock, with a 4.57 metre big hand, was reputed to be the world's third-largest clock in 1912.

The massive clock dominated the centre of Vancouver. When it was built, the prestige building featured oak door frames and marble stairways. Dominic built solid buildings. According to his nephew Frank Farrell, "he liked good buildings. He wouldn't put them up unless they were tops."

In the First World War, Dominic served overseas in army supply, delivering beef and pork to the forces serving in France. When he returned, he continued his various business ventures. Besides owning Burns Bog, he owned a number of other farms and property in Vancouver, Victoria, Seattle and Nelson.

Small but strong, mentally and physically, Dominic was much like his older brother Pat in his love of "horse trading." According to F. W. Trounce, Dominic "would rather make $25 on a 'trade' than put through a 'deal' which might make ten times the money." Both brothers were frugal and disliked public exposure— even more so in Dominic's case as he stuttered. Dominic shared another trait with his brother as both Burns quietly contributed to various charities.

Dominic remained a bachelor all his life and died in Vancouver in 1933 at age 74. His body is buried in Ocean View Park.

Peat Harvesting in Burns Bog

Peat harvesting began in Burns Bog in the 1930s but initial attempts proved unsuccessful, as well as very expensive, with one company expending $300,000 before ceasing operation. Another company, Atkins and Durbrow Ltd., later took over the operation.

A series of German aerial raids on London in World War II started a chain of events which led to a boom in peat harvesting on Burns Bog. German bombers dropped magnesium fire bombs on London, with devastating results. The Allies decided to counter with their own fire bombs. In Nevada, the U.S.

began constructing a $60 million magnesium munitions operation. Peat played a vital part as a catalytic agent in the refining of magnesium. As American sources were unable to supply enough peat, the U.S. approached Western Peat, a Canadian company.

Western Peat began a massive construction program in Burns Bog, building a processing plant, roads and ditches. Sixteen kilometres of railway were laid in the bog to access the 648 hectares opened for peat harvesting. Annual production was a million bales, with each bale weighing 36 kilograms.

Two peat-processing plants operated during the war, one built on the east side of the bog in 1942 and another erected on the west side two years later. One plant used a hydraulic method, employing powerful hoses to blast the peat loose. The peat then floated along a series of ditches to a sump. From there, the peat slurry was pumped to the plant. Inside the plant, a series of machines, similar to those involved in converting pulp to paper with roller presses, squeezed the water out. Next the peat was dried and finally baled.

After the war, Western Peat bought out Atkins and Durbrow's 400 hectare holdings, remaining as the only peat operator working the bog for some years. Western Peat went on to become the largest peat producer in North America, at one time operating six plants across Canada. Peat harvesting on a large scale continued in the 1950s and 1960s.

Over the decades of peat harvesting stretching back to the 1930s, different methods of peat removal were used. Initially, the peat was hand harvested. Workers cut peat "plugs," measuring 30 to 40 centimetres wide and about 1.5 metres long, stacking the plugs to dry in the sun and air. This method left long striations. Later, machines mechanically removed the top layer of peat, which was then dried.

Water barges gave way to a large hovercraft in the 1970s. A clamshell digger mounted at one end of the hovercraft excavated the peat mechanically, transferring it to a hopper built on the air-floating barge for initial processing. Then the peat slurry was piped to the plant to be dried and bagged. Another method, discussed above, used an extensive high-pressure hose system.

Today there remains little trace of the once booming peat operation, which employed 1,500 workers during its peak. The large peat plant at the eastern edge of Burns Bog has been demolished. The extensive piping system is slowly being swallowed by the bog. Parts of the narrow-gauge railway line remain. One old engine and several cars used to carry the peat lie abandoned, rusting away. The large hovercraft also lies derelict, its clamshell digger removed, rusting and listing as it slowly sinks into the peat it once removed.

The large, central part of the bog, owned by Western Delta Lands, lies unused, except for a local gun club which hunts waterfowl. Delta police have a firing range and they train in this area. Occasionally this area is used for practising helicopter landings.

The central portion of the bog is "class 7" agricultural land, the least desirable rating for agriculture. Cranberries require bog-type soils and Burns Bog is ideal for this type of production. In 1993 Ocean Spray, which controls almost 90 percent of the cranberry market, brought part of the bog into production. Most of the cranberry and blueberry operations take place along the fringes of the bog.

British Columbia produces the world's third-largest cranberry crop. Only Massachusetts and Wisconsin harvest more. In 1996 the cranberry crop amounted to $21 million.

In only a century of European settlement, the Fraser delta has undergone a profound environmental transformation. Once a wilderness of river, marshes and shore, the delta has been logged, diked and drained. Railways, roads and ditches slash across the landscape. Housing tracts and farms neatly section the delta.

Visible even from space, one large piece of the original ecosystem remains—Burns Bog is still wild and wet.

The Peat Operation in the 1940s

Hauling The peat trains load up at the stockpiles and haul the dry blocks into the factory. Each car holds enough for some 50 bales.

The growing Lower Mainland population threatens Burns Bog. Don DeMille photo.

Chapter Ten

Development Threatens Burns Bog

"Burns Bog ... (is) threatened by golf course proposals, garbage dumps, landfills and other development. I urge your government to protect Burns Bog from destruction."

Dr. Helen Caldicott
*in a letter to former
Prime Minister Mulroney*

Despite Burns Bog's remarkable ability to survive decades of abuse, enormous pressures threaten its future. Government can offer little protection, as most of the bog is privately owned. Past mega-project proposals have ranged from an immense $10.5 billion port/town project to an 800 hectare horse race course. Numerous golf course proposals still await planning permission.

As the largest undeveloped urban land mass in any city in Canada, Burns Bog has been the target of a number of mega-project development proposals. Ironically, while all these proposals were defeated, the numerous small encroachments eating away at Burns Bog could destroy it. Private landfills, drainage canals, tree clearing and unauthorized dumping slowly erode the fringes of the bog. Left unchecked, these pinpricks, as one environmentalist warns, "could bleed the bog to death, like that old saying: How can an ant kill a snake? By a thousand small bites." To many "boggites" or defenders of Burns Bog, piecemeal destruction of the bog ranks as the greatest threat against the bog. Big issues draw a big response, while slowly the fringes of Burns Bog erode away.

Some examples of smaller incursions include: the municipality carving a wide drainage channel from one end of the bog to the other; Delta approving bulldozing of 32.4 hectares for a cranberry field; the construction of a radio tower; clearcutting on private land along the edge of the bog; and the province issuing permits for dumpsites along the northern edge of the bog.

The overall amount of demolition, land clearing and construction waste, called DLC waste, was estimated at a staggering 830,000 tonnes in 1993, half of that amount ending up in private landfills. DLC waste makes up about a third of the total waste generated in the GVRD annually. A number of private landfill companies operate along River Road. When Delta refused to issue permits for demolition waste, the province did. There is no daily check on the amount dumped and some of these private landfills dump in excess of their permits.

"We're like traffic cops, we catch one out of every 100 or so," admits Fred Barnes, the environment ministry's head of industrial investigations. And when officials do cite a violator, the courts rarely impose anything but small fines.

When Delta amended a soil bylaw, to curb demolition landfilling, Western Delta Lands sued the Corporation of Delta. WDL contended the restrictions prevent the company from backfilling its peat extractions. Tom Johnson, vice-president of WDL at the time, said the amendment was made in bad faith, effectively devaluing the company's land, as peat extraction is no longer viable under the restriction. "As a result, the land is difficult to sell and reduced in market value."

WDL vice-president Johnson went on to say that if the company is not allowed to backfill, the excavated land would be dangerous to the public. Burns Bog supporters contend that backfilling with demolition material or gravel after peat is harvested would not only destroy the bog but would prepare the bog for future development.

A gas line running parallel to River Road shifted and geo-technical experts determined landfill dumping had pushed the gas pipeline 3 metres out of position. BC Gas and the landfill owners could not agree initially on who would pay for the repairs and replacement pipe. One landfill company, concerned about a possible explosion, applied to the Ministry of Environment to increase their dumping limit to stabilize the ground around the pipeline. Eliza Olson, president of the Burns Bog Conservation Society, questioned the logic of the application when dumping had caused the problem in the first place. "You can't dump on bogs without destroying them."

Driving along River Road next to the Fraser River, a series of flat-topped hills of rubble, some 25 metres high, rise up to dwarf the bog to the south. Fleets of trucks carrying demolition waste dump their loads. Bulldozers compact these mountains of refuse, preparing them for industrial sites. One company, Alpha Manufacturing, disputed an environment ministry advisory to stop dumping. According to the ministry, Alpha exceeded its limit of 900,000 cubic metres of demolition construction material.

Alpha president Taffy Anderson contends much of the volume is air, which escapes when the waste is compacted by bulldozers. What arrives as a 2 metre load of waste can easily be flattened to centimetres when compacted by a bulldozer. This debate over whether "air is waste" might sound frivolous, but the stakes are high as Alpha faced a fine of up to $1 million.

Paul George, of the Western Canada Wilderness Committee, called the increase in private dumps "insane." He explained, "It's really accelerated in the last few years [with] truckloads and truckloads going in there with all kinds of junk from demolished houses."

The issue of responsibility is complicated, as municipal, provincial and federal agencies have jurisdiction and responsibilities in various areas. For example, the provincial Ministry of Environment issues permits for private landfills. The dumps are theoretically subject to municipal bylaws. But should toxic material leak into the Fraser River to harm fish, the federal government would become involved.

The political landscape surrounding the bog is as confusing as the tangle of jurisdictions. Even with a supposedly "pro-bog" civic and provincial government in power, environmentalists contend little has been done to back up election slogans. Delta mayor Beth Johnson led a slate that claimed "Delta needs the green space of the bog, which is an important biological feature of the Fraser estuary." In the 1993 election campaign, Johnson's slate promised "to work with the provincial government to preserve Burns Bog as a unique natural area."

Yet mayor Johnson reintroduced a proposal for a golf course on the bog after it was defeated the previous summer. What changed the minds of several Delta councillors was a provincial recommendation by the environment ministry. "Any time the province says a project is not only not a problem but actually complements the environment, that has to be persuasive," said veteran Delta councillor Bruce McDonald. But the provincial NDP at their 1990 assembly called for a "moratorium [on] Burns Bog and all ALR lands south of the south arm of the Fraser River and east around Boundary Bay."

Norm Lortie, the former provincial MLA for Delta North, agreed that a moratorium is necessary: "I don't think we should be allowing any development until we've done a complete ecological study of the whole area known as the bog."

Both levels of government blame each other, with Delta mayor Johnson claiming to want to preserve the bog but that "there's not much we can do to preserve the bog, given so much of it is somebody's private land."

The province negotiated for over a year with Western Delta Lands, the company that owns much of Burns Bog. The NDP government offered $27.5 million for a south-central portion of the bog.

"There's a big difference between what the province says it's worth and what it's worth," said Western Delta Lands vice-president Nick Westeinde when rejecting the offer. "We won't sell unless we get fair market value."

The proposed South Fraser Perimeter Road Project is one of the major potential threats to the future of the bog. The four-lane highway will follow the south side of the Fraser River through the neighbouring City of Surrey. Delta is behind Surrey in terms of studies, hearings and purchasing rights-of-way. Delta faces a major environmental hurdle as the highway will cut through Burns Bog. The federal government promised to pump money into the highway, as the South Fraser Perimeter Road would stimulate the economy. A two-year study claims the new highway would generate over $700 million in investment in industrial plants and other facilities.

Opponents fear the highway will slice deep into the bog, which would open the bog to development. Even if the highway follows the existing River Road, the easy access would certainly add to the pressure facing the municipality to develop the bog. When North Delta residents were asked for input on an area plan for North Delta, their responses indicated they disapproved of widening River Road. These results suggest a highway would not be popular.

Perhaps this is why Delta, after cost sharing a $347,000 study with the province, presented only a two-lane version of the plan at a series of public meetings in 1995. Following the open house meetings designed to gauge public support, Delta politicians agreed to expanding the study to include four lanes. Two Delta councillors raised concerns.

"It seems to be a bigger and bigger concept every time we hear about it," said Delta councillor Wendy Jeske. Added fellow councillor Krista Engelland, "I had a feeling the scope of the project would broaden to four lanes and I'm not happy with that at all." Extra public meetings were scheduled to focus on the four-lane option.

Other pressures cloud the future of the bog. The Katzie band, part of the Sto:lo First Nations, recently launched a land claim that includes Burns Bog. "The government has acknowledged that aboriginal people have lived here since time immemorial, so we don't have to document every tree and rock," says Barbara Wyss, who researched the band's claim.

The Katzie coexisted with other aboriginal people, including the Musqueam, Tsawwassen, Langley and Sto:lo bands. The overlapping claims of the various bands will be negotiated by the Treaty Commission, a group set up to settle land claims in B.C. The Treaty Commission consists of aboriginal as well as provincial and federal government representatives.

The bog survives despite overwhelming pressure.   *Don DeMille photo.*

In this "preserve or develop" dilemma, one of the fundamental questions is whether the bog is worth saving. According to Dr. Richard Hebda, "Burns Bog is an exceptional ecological phenomenon of international significance. As naturalists it is our collective responsibility to ensure this natural legacy survives."

First Nations Claim Burns Bog

While settlers in most provinces entered into treaties with the original people, this was not the case in British Columbia. The first white settlers did not sign treaties with the majority of the province's aboriginal inhabitants, leading to legal wrangling that has festered for over a century. At stake is legal title to most of the province of British Columbia, including Vancouver and most of the Lower Mainland—some of the most expensive real estate in Canada.

A number of First Nations, in filing claims with the B.C. Treaty Commission, claim Burns Bog as part of their traditional territory. The five-member commission was established in 1993 to represent federal, provincial and aboriginal interests. Given the high stakes and complex issues involved, the three-way talks over land claims could take years to resolve.

Private property is not on the table, according to statements by former Premier Harcourt, although provincial and federal land might be used as part of a settlement—as well as cash compensation. Chilliwack mayor John Les, president of the Federation of Canadian Municipalities, says both federal and provincial levels of government "have reassured us all along that fee simple title, your house or mine, is not on the table."

Katzie researcher Barbara Wyss concedes that regaining traditional territory would be difficult. "We're not looking at displacing people from their homes. Rather, where possible, the governments are looking at where Crown land is available." Katzie chief Diane Bailey echoes this: "It would be great if we could get land somewhere."

KATZIE INDIAN BAND: The Pitt Meadows-based band has a registered population of about 350 members. Most members live on five reserves, including one on Barnston Island in the Fraser River. Today many of the band members follow their traditional past by being active in the commercial fishery. The band's ancestral territory includes Surrey, New Westminster and Vancouver. The Katzie's land was also used by the Tsawwassen, Musqueam and Sto:lo—who are also negotiating land claims.

MUSQUEAM INDIAN BAND: The band has nearly 1,000 members , which includes some 450 members living on three reserves. The band claims all of Greater Vancouver as its traditional territory.

SQUAMISH INDIAN BAND: This large band has a membership of more than 2,500, over half of whom reside on eight reserves, including one in Squamish and another in North Vancouver. The Squamish claim Howe Sound and Greater Vancouver.

STO:LO NATION: The Sto:lo, or People of the River, is made up of 18 smaller native bands in the Fraser Valley. The alliance has nearly 2,000 members, over half living on reserves. The Sto:lo have lived along the Fraser River from its ocean mouth to the canyons at Yale. Their claim includes Greater Vancouver and the entire Lower Mainland as their territory.

TSAWWASSEN INDIAN BAND: This small band has under 200 members. The band claims the Greater Vancouver region south of the Fraser and the Gulf Islands as their traditional territory.

A landfill between Burns Bog and the city.   *Don DeMille photo.*

Chapter Eleven

Eco Time Bomb

"Vancouver profits while Delta stinks."
Environmental slogan

 Vancouver is proud of its 400 hectare Stanley Park, the jewel of its park system. Stanley Park is the largest urban park in Canada, located only minutes from downtown Vancouver, offering Vancouverites an escape from concrete and glass towers to a natural haven with highrise firs and cedars. Visitors to this prime example of a West Coast rainforest are amazed that such a large expanse of forest escaped development. In 1989 Stanley Park was declared a national historic site.

While Vancouverites enjoy a taste of wilderness in the middle of a large city, at the same time they are dumping their garbage in a landfill larger than Stanley Park. The GVRD's huge dump, the largest west of Toronto, takes approximately 25 percent of the Lower Mainland's garbage. Vancouver owns the dump and charges other municipalities who use it. Vancouver makes $11 million a year on the dump. The municipality of Delta is caught in the same conflict-of-interest issue, as their share in the annual royalties is $800,000. Since the dump opened, Vancouver has made close to $100 million from it.

The Greater Vancouver Regional District's landfill, situated on the southwestern corner of the bog, jeopardizes the future of Burns Bog. If Stanley Park is the jewel of Vancouver, Burns Bog is a rough diamond that is being buried under tons of garbage.

Imagine the outcry from Vancouverites if garbage were to be dumped in Stanley Park. Yet thousands of tons are trucked to Burns Bog every day, covering this wilderness jewel.

Environmentalists contend the dump is an "eco time bomb," as it sprawls on unstable land and leaks toxic chemicals. Other privately owned dumps exist on the bog, including a chemical storage site and numerous small dumps. All of these landfills threaten to destroy the unique ecosystem that is Burns Bog.

Any contamination of the bog potentially threatens vital salmon runs on the Fraser River north of the bog and Boundary Bay to the south. Each year the Fraser River supports enormous runs of all species of Pacific salmon, including the largest sockeye salmon run in the world.

The B.C. Ministry of Environment requires that new landfills or expansions of existing ones not be located on or near unstable ground. Yet the bog lies in an earthquake zone. The unstable land shifted a natural gas pipeline, forcing BC Gas to shut it down.

"Vancouver profits while Delta stinks," is more than a popular ecoslogan; the phrase neatly sums up the dilemma. The municipality of Delta more or less gave away the land to Vancouver, which owns and operates the landfill. Delta only charged the GVRD a token fee. The rationale behind the give-away was simple—Delta dumps its garbage free and shares in the profits generated by the fees paid by other municipalities. Unfortunately, the residents of North Delta are left with an ever-growing mountain of garbage.

The sight of this mountain of garbage is not exactly a tourist attraction. Nor is the smell, which in the past led residents to protest.

The GVRD adopted a solid waste management plan in 1995 which targeted as its goal a 50 percent reduction in the area's per capita garbage production. Unfortunately, the Greater Vancouver area is the fastest-growing region in Canada. The 100,000 new residents each year will only increase the overall amount of garbage. Already the landfill receives 400,000 tonnes of garbage a year.

Peter Brady, the project manager of the solid waste management plan review, admits, "all waste management options affect communities and the environment. Landfills produce methane gas and can produce leachates which may contaminate soil and water resources."

Leachate is the liquid waste that runs off from landfills. Acids from food mix with other waste material to form an acidic liquid. Other materials, like PCBs, dioxins, lead and arsenic, are not degraded by any biological process and rainwater flushes these toxic substances from the compacted landfill. To handle this toxic runoff, Burns Bog landfill employs a dual ditch system consisting of

Business as usual at the landfill   *Don DeMille photo.*

an inner and outer ditch to collect any contaminated water escaping from the landfill. The inner dike is designed to collect the leachate that percolates through the waste after a rain. This liquid is pumped to the Annacis Island treatment plant.

Unfortunately, samples of the discharge from the Annacis plant on the Fraser have proven toxic, "putting both fish and wildlife at risk," according to a warning issued by the federal fisheries minister of the day, Brian Tobin. He wrote the GVRD, warning them to take action to upgrade the sewage treatment plant or face charges under the Fisheries Act. Tobin's action came just a day after the Fraser River was named the most endangered river in British Columbia by the Outdoor Recreation Council of B.C. The Annacis Island plant is the worst repeat offender for municipal sewage pollution, racking up a dozen citations for dumping toxic sewage into the Fraser River.

The outer ditch surrounding the landfill at Burns Bog flows to Crescent Slough and eventually into the Fraser River. This outer ditch has been "found to be toxic" according to a Ministry of Environment memo (file # 50.150103). Another potential problem is the seepage of leachate under the ditches.

A very real concern is the garbage itself. Experts consider over one percent of household waste as hazardous. Tests by the federal government found dioxins and PCBs in waste material. These substances are so toxic even traces can be fatal to humans. These substances can eventually work their way into the food chain, besides showing up in leachate. A rat or gull scavenging at the landfill can carry the toxic substances or be eaten by a predator.

The GVRD landfill is not the only waste site affecting the bog. Numerous small, private landfills are adjacent to the bog. The GVRD solid waste plan review of 1993 reports that approximately 415,000 tonnes of demolition, land clearing and construction waste ended up in private and often poorly regulated landfills in Delta and Richmond. The amount of DLC waste equals the amount of garbage dumped annually in the GVRD landfill.

Long considered a wasteland, Burns Bog has been used as a dump for years in one form or other. Back in the 1960s, waste produced by Dow Chemical Canada Inc. was used as fill for a road in Burns Bog. The gravel-topped road is an extension of 60th Avenue and is between 1 and 1.5 kilometres long. The gravel road leads to a number of sheds used to store explosives.

Gulls fight for morsels over the swamp.   *Don DeMille photo.*

Flotsam in a perimeter ditch.   *Don DeMille photo.*

The toxic material from Dow is called reactor-mass, the residue of a chemical process. The sludge contains the remains of phenols and benzoic acid. The wastes came from a plant Dow operated in Delta from the early 1960s to the mid-1980s that manufactured chemicals used in glues, food additives and herbicides. Dow says it does not know exactly how the chemicals got there.

In 1985 the provincial and municipal authorities were aware of the chemical waste material. As B.C. had nowhere to store the material, no attempt was made to move the toxic residue and it remained where it was. A quick fix in the mid-1980s simply covered the area with more fill and gravel. Hiding the problem provided only a temporary solution. Within a few years, the rain had exposed the chemical waste at the side of the road. In 1992, Tanya Lebans, a communications officer with Dow, said the company would do whatever was necessary to clean up the private road. Four years later, nothing had been done.

The waste material is dark, with a greenish tinge. The partially crystallized waste gives off a chemical odour and glints in bare peat more than 10 metres from the road. Besides the trace levels of phenols and benzoic acid found in the waste, copper and cobalt were also found.

After a quarter-century, the various chemicals could have reacted or degraded into other products.

A walk along the "toxic road" reveals a death zone extending some distance. Bodies of fish float in the stream by the road. A former environment ministry manager confirmed that a small stream by the road had no life in it for 900 metres. Near the road, a row of sheds storing explosives offers a surreal counterpoint.

A Garbage Primer

✔ Per capita, we throw out nearly a metric tonne of waste each year.

✔ That amounts to over 2.4 million tonnes of solid waste every year in the GVRD (1993 figures).

✔ About 60 percent of the solid waste is trucked to landfills. There are only a few landfills, the Port Mann in Surrey, the Burns Bog landfill and the Cache Creek site, 300 km from Vancouver. Trash is trucked to Burns Bog, compacted by a bulldozer and finally covered with soil.

✔ Burns Bog landfill site, owned by the City of Vancouver, sprawls over 627 hectares of the bog. Only 268 hectares of the landfill are currently being used. The dump has been open for business since 1964 and is expected to handle waste for another half-century. After the landfill closes 50 years from now, it will take another 25 to 30 years for the site to stabilize enough to be built on.

✔ Burns Bog takes in about 400,000 metric tonnes of waste each year.

✔ Burns Bog landfill has a two-dike system consisting of an inner and outer dike. The inner dike is designed to collect the leachate that percolates through the waste. This is pumped to the Annacis Island sewage treatment plant.

On a hike in September of 1996, we stop near the cluster of sheds. One trailer at the unguarded site has a large hole in its tailgate, large enough for a person to climb through. Within easy reach are a number of boxes. They could contain anything.

Small wonder Burns Bog is called an "eco time bomb."

Protesters Fight To Save Bog

On September 23, 1994, a dozen protesters chained themselves to garbage trucks to block the entrance to Burns Bog landfill.

Their blockade shut down the landfill for three hours. "We've had protesters at the landfill entrance before," said Brian Davies, assistant city engineer. "Normally, they just advertise their cause. It's unusual for them to block the road."

The dozen protesters support Earth First. Their news release stated, "Disgusted with the continued destruction of Lower Mainland wetland areas and the gross overconsumption of industrial society, Earth First has launched a major industrial action campaign to save Burns Bog, Boundary Bay, Surrey Bend and any other remaining fragments of wilderness left in the Lower Mainland."

Delta police arrested 10 of the protesters, charging 5 with public mischief. Amy Newton was one of those arrested.

"Anything is worth it to save the bog," she said.

"Burns Bog is being destroyed by this landfill," another protester, Fiona Moorhead, claimed. "It's an amazing natural refuge and we're dumping tons and tons of garbage into it."

Eagles roost in Burns Bog cottonwoods.　　　　　　　　　*Don DeMille photo.*

Chapter Twelve

Peatlands Counteract Global Warming

"Peatlands play a positive role in addressing the global problem of atmospheric carbon dioxide."

State of Forestry in Canada report

Imagine Vancouver 20 years from now. Greater Vancouver's population has soared to 3.5 million, with industrial development keeping pace. Housing clusters perch high up the mountains overlooking the city. Urban sprawl has crept up the Fraser Valley. Now tracts of housing almost reach Hope. Much of the fertile Fraser Valley has been paved over to accommodate the new expressway system, constantly clogged with over 2 million vehicles.

Burns Bog has finally been developed: the outer fringes are industrial sites and the inner portion is an enormous new suburb of almost 200,000 people named West Delta. An eight-lane expressway opened up what the developer termed "a wasteland," although a small portion of bog was saved as a nature park.

All this uncontrolled growth has come with a price. World-wide increases in cars and industry have led to a slight rise in the average global temperature. And what's wrong with Vancouverites basking in a warmer climate? Unfortunately, temperatures would not be the only thing to rise in this future scenario. Another by-product would be an increase in sea levels. Richmond and Boundary Bay are especially vulnerable and would require extensive diking to keep out the sea. Another unwanted by-product of global warming would be an increase in spring flooding along rivers such as the Fraser, as mountain glaciers melt down.

Imagine the impact this future scenario would have on renewable resources. As global temperatures rise, salmon stocks would decrease because West Coast salmon are extremely sensitive to any increase in temperatures. Even a minor change in temperatures could produce a profound effect on ecosystems like the Fraser River, the world's largest salmon river. "Economically, the effects would be catastrophic," predicted then B.C. Minister of Environment, Moe Sihota, in 1995. "The salmon industry runs the risk of being a footnote in the history books," former federal environment minister Sheila Copps warned while discussing global warming.

What's at stake just in the salmon fishery alone provides a chilling warning. B.C.'s fishing industry now provides jobs for about 25,000 British Columbians. The value of both the commercial and recreational fisheries totals almost $2 billion a year.

But will we be able to count on this renewable resource? For more than 400 years, cod was caught off Canada's east coast. No one took the warnings of a collapse seriously—until it happened. The Atlantic fishery crashed partly due to global warming. That catastrophe could be repeated on the west coast.

What is especially ominous about global warming is the prediction some scientists make that it's already too late to halt the warming trend, as greenhouse gases remain in the atmosphere for decades. One of the prime greenhouse gases is carbon dioxide. Canadians pump more carbon dioxide into the atmosphere on a per capita rate than people in any other country except the United States.

A closer look at Greater Vancouver 20 years from now reveals another downside. This second damaging side-effect is very much "localized"—the smog that clouds Vancouver's future. Cars emit carbon dioxide into the atmosphere. Doubling the number of vehicles doubles the problem. As Louise Comeau, a specialist in climate change with the Sierra Club of Canada, warns: "It's not inconceivable that treating the atmosphere as the world's largest garbage dump is already having an impact on the environment."

What exactly would this enlarged version of present-day Vancouver look like? From the new West Delta mega-development that was once Burns Bog, you would not see any mountains, due to a brown smudge hanging over the city. Imagine a city shrouded in smog, and the accompanying rise in respiratory ailments.

Tourism would fall and health costs rise. Medical experts agree the foul chemical soup would lead to an increase in the number of premature deaths. Emergency department visits for those suffering from asthma, chronic bronchitis, emphysema and lung disorders would also increase.

Ground-level ozone pollution is thought to be the second-greatest contributor to lung disease after smoking. Ozone is a three-atom molecule of oxygen which, in the stratosphere, screens out ultraviolet radiation which would destroy life on Earth. But closer to the ground, ozone is a major component of smog. Combined with oxides of nitrogen and soot, it is a toxic corrosive. Certain particles in smog have been linked to cancer.

Vancouver could expect more "killer smogs." Even today Vancouver has experienced five-day "ozone episodes" and more poisonous smogs are predicted given the region's unusual geography. The mountains ringing the Lower Mainland on three sides form a natural trap and breezes from the Pacific prevent any air escaping to the west.

The combination of offshore currents and temperature inversions create a "lid," which cooks the petrochemical soup within the area's 4,800 square kilometre valley.

Vancouverites should look elsewhere to see how other cities handle smog emergencies. When Mexico City declares a "smog emergency," the city grinds to a standstill. Cars are ordered off the streets, factories must cut production by two-thirds and schools close.

Other major cities like Athens, Los Angeles and London have had to enforce emergency measures to reduce "killer smogs"—so-called because thousands can die from respiratory illnesses.

Cities with severe smog suffer from more than just health problems. The particulates in the air eventually "fall" and damage crops. The Fraser Valley's fertile delta is especially vulnerable. Already the Lower Mainland's one million cars account for three-quarters of the area's pollution. In 1990 that amounted to over 600,000 tonnes of pollutants released into the air. According to the GVRD, that is equivalent to filling BC Place Stadium 390 times. Small wonder that on some days Vancouver's smog is worse than Los Angeles'.

The burning of fossil fuels in cars is not only a regional problem, it is one of the major contributors to global warming. What have cars and bogs got in common? Until recently, the vital role bogs play in combating this threat was poorly understood.

Carbon dioxide ranks as the major gas contributing to global warming. While bogs cover only approximately 2 to 3 percent of the Earth, the peat contained in bogs holds enormous amounts of carbon. Disrupting peatlands causes two unwanted effects. First, by releasing carbon dioxide and methane into the atmosphere, both gases contribute to the greenhouse effect, warming our Earth. And second, a drained bog no longer helps cool the Earth.

Richard Hebda says, "Wetland areas hold carbons, and we want that carbon to stay there. We don't want it released, which is another reason why the bog is important ecologically."

Hebda goes on to explain: "Burns Bog provides one of the very few ways of scrubbing carbon dioxide from our atmosphere. Bog plants convert atmospheric carbon dioxide to plant matter, which upon their death is permanently stored as peat."

By acting as carbon sinks, bogs play a passive but positive role in counteracting global warming. "Draining the bog or burying it leads to peat decomposition and release of carbon and methane, a very potent greenhouse gas," warns Hebda. Forestry Canada estimates about 15 percent of the world's organic carbon is stored in peatlands, while forests hold only 8 percent.

Disturb peatlands and these greenhouse gases will escape, speeding up global warming. Canada bears a heavy responsibility as our country holds a quarter of the world's wetland area. Canada's vast wetlands cover 14 percent of the country. More than 90 percent of these are peatlands.

A State of Forestry in Canada report states: "The greatest proportion of carbon is stored in peatlands, which comprise about 60 percent of the stored carbon. Peatlands clearly play a positive role in addressing the global problem of atmospheric carbon dioxide."

According to one controversial theory, bogs trigger ice ages. As bogs expand, they suck carbon out of the atmosphere, and trap carbon in peat, cooling down Earth like gigantic air conditioners. Bogs work to cool the planet in other, more subtle ways. For example, bogs reflect twice as much sunlight as forests and up to eight times the amount when they are snow covered. Bogs also trap water, which can only evaporate, since bogs allow little escape to a river. This increases the cloud cover to reflect even more sun. As they grow, according to this scientific scenario, bogs tip the climate into an ice age.

Are bogs powerful enough to plunge the Earth into an ice age? One way to find out is to extract air bubbles contained in cores of ancient ice. Drilling deep into the ice in Russia and elsewhere shows that carbon dioxide levels were 25 to 30 percent lower in glacial eras. In other words, in an ice age a reverse greenhouse effect occurs. Examination of air trapped in ice cores reveals that the amount of carbon dioxide is inversely proportional to the amount of peatland covering the planet at the time. Another technique that uses fossilized peat indicates bogs covered extensive areas during the ice ages, perhaps 20 percent of the Earth's surface.

How exactly do bogs reduce the level of carbon dioxide in the air? To understand the role of bogs, first we must look at carbon—one of the basic building blocks of life. Considered the most important chemical element, carbon has the unique ability to form complex compounds. The number of known compounds exceeds a million.

The amount of carbon in the Earth's atmosphere in the form of carbon dioxide is about equal to the amount in living matter—which is mostly trees. But the wild card is the carbon in the Earth's soil stored as dead organic material. This amount exceeds the atmospheric carbon by several times. Over time, bacteria decompose this carbon into greenhouse gases such as methane, nitrous oxide and carbon dioxide.

The Earth's climate is also dependent on the level of carbon dioxide in the atmosphere, which traps heat and keeps the planet warm. Change the amount of this gas cycling through the planet and the climate changes.

Carbon circulates throughout the Earth, from the atmosphere to the sea floor. This carbon cycle is complex but critical to life as we know it. Even before plants existed, volcanoes spewed carbon dioxide into the air. Water in the atmosphere dissolved this gas to form carbonic acid, which fell with rainwater. The carbonic acid ate away at rock, creating calcium and bicarbonate. Rains washed these compounds into rivers and eventually into the ocean. Organisms such as plankton in the sea used bicarbonate to build shells. When the shells died, they fell to the ocean floor and turned to limestone. As ocean sediments built up, carbonate was compressed deep into the Earth. When this gets hot, carbon dioxide is released and the gas is vented during volcanic eruptions, completing the cycle of carbon.

Plants speed up this cycle in two ways. All living plants take in carbon dioxide from the air and transform the gas to oxygen and organic compounds. This process is called photosynthesis. The carbon is also absorbed into the living material of plants and becomes tissue, which eventually becomes material for fossil fuels.

When plants or trees die, microbes decompose the remains, using oxygen in the soil and releasing carbon dioxide. Bogs function differently, interrupting the usual cycle of nature—growth, death, decomposition and rebirth. In bogs, decay is delayed often for thousands of years. Plants die but do not decay because there is little oxygen to aid the bacteria breaking down the plants.

Also, the acidic and waterlogged nature of a bog prevents decomposition. Over the centuries, organic material piles up, layer upon layer, trapping the carbon. This forms peat, or "young coal." If left long enough, and compressed over centuries, the peat changes to coal.

Sphagnum moss is the dominant bog plant. This mini-moss is so primitive it never evolved roots and grows at the slow rate of about 2 millimetres a year. Yet it rules the bog. Functioning like a sponge, it traps water in its cells. Slowly expanding, tangled mats of sphagnum make the soil acidic and kill off competition.

Burns Bog is a raised-dome bog and the upper portion is not permanently waterlogged so decay there is aerobic, as oxygen breaks down living plant

Blooms beneath the bridge. *Don DeMille photo.*

material. Below this upper layer is an anaerobic lower layer where waterlogged conditions retard decay or decomposition.

Functioning as the lungs of the Lower Mainland, Burns Bog directly affects our quality of life. Locally, Burns Bog helps to maintain air quality by absorbing greenhouse gases and also by cooling the atmosphere. Burns Bog functions as a gigantic carbon sink, absorbing carbon dioxide from the atmosphere and releasing oxygen to counteract global warming. The bog also provides cool and moisture-laden air for the region. Thus Burns Bog serves as a natural and positive defence against global warming.

Global warming is a complex process involving "greenhouse" gases; including carbon dioxide, methane, chlorofluorocarbons, nitrous oxide and other gases, which interact to cause our atmosphere to heat up. Anyone who has gotten into a car after it sat in direct sun on a hot day has experienced the greenhouse effect. Glass windows allow sunlight in but trap heat reflected off the seats and dashboard. The Earth's atmosphere works in the same way. About 40 percent of the sun's light is absorbed by the Earth's surface. The shield in the atmosphere is composed of various gases. Water vapour and carbon dioxide make up about half the greenhouse shield. Methane, nitrous oxide, ozone and other gases make up the rest. This gas shield traps outgoing heat.

The onset of the industrial age, about 200 years ago, marked the start of the escalation of carbon dioxide levels as fossil fuels such as coal, oil and gas were used to generate energy. Over the past century, carbon dioxide levels increased 25 percent. Over the same period, deforestation has increased. Because forests absorb carbon dioxide, destruction of forests adds to the problem. To complicate the overall picture, heating up of the Earth and acid rain have led to an increase in forest fires, which compounds the problem by leading to more global warming. As global warming accelerates, ocean levels will rise, threatening two-thirds of Earth's wetlands.

Population is a huge contributor as the number of humans skyrockets past five billion. Only 50 years ago, the world population was around two billion. Today, the planet's human inhabitants have created a greater demand for food, which in turn has led to loss of forests, draining of wetlands and increased pollution as farmers increase the amount of chemicals used to produce more crops. Animal species decline as natural habitat is used to feed all the extra mouths.

Each year some 6.5 billion tonnes of carbon are released into the atmosphere. Most of this carbon, some 4.8 billion tonnes, comes from fossil fuel emissions. Deforestation and altering land use accounts for much of the rest of the carbon. Vehicles contribute the majority of the fossil-fuel emissions. While there were only 50 million autos in 1960, by the year 2000 the figure will rise to 500 million. These rocketing trends become even more of a concern as scientists believe there is a delay of about 25 years as carbon and other gases mix in the atmosphere. In other words, even if we stop pumping carbon into the atmosphere, the slow response time will mean that temperatures will continue to increase for a quarter-century as the carbon slowly mingles.

Whatever the causes, there is no doubt the Earth's temperatures are heading upward. Records for the "hottest years" tumble almost annually. In 1995, the Earth's average temperature reached 15.38°C, the hottest since records began in the 1860s. Climatologist Eric Taylor of Environment Canada said Vancouver averaged 11°C in 1995, its second-warmest average temperature. The 10 warmest years over the last 130 years have occurred in the 1980s and 1990s.

In the past 150 years, glaciers in the Rocky Mountains have shrunk about 25 percent. This dramatic reduction is evidence of a warming climate according to geographer Brian Luckman. "Glaciers are sensitive to changes in temperature and precipitation. Long-term changes in glacier characteristics obviously reflect longer-term changes in climate."

Overall, the 20th century was one degree warmer than the 19th century. By the end of the 21st century, some scientists predict the Earth's average temperature might be 5°C warmer—hotter than any time over the past million years.

Vital Reports, a British publication, reports that in 1995 carbon emissions from the burning of fossil fuels also reached a record high. Floods of record severity, hurricanes, forest fires and other indicators of changing climate accompanied the record average temperature in 1995. Already the economic consequences are being felt as insurance companies report that weather damage claims have tripled since the 1980s, following a period of violent storms. A heat wave in the United States was partly responsible for the smallest grain harvest since the late 1980s.

Another little-known ecological crisis is happening over part of the oceans, which cover 75 percent of the world. Holes in the Arctic and Antarctic ozone shields mean the sun's ultraviolet rays can now reach the ocean. Phytoplankton have no skin to protect themselves against these ultraviolet rays. Besides their vital role in the food chain, these phytoplankton absorb the most carbon and produce the world's greatest amount of oxygen.

One example of runaway carbon build-up is Venus. About the same size and composition as Earth, Venus is 450°C warmer. The dry rock surface is hot enough to melt lead. The reason why Venus is so hot is the amount of carbon dioxide in its atmosphere. The high levels trap 100 times the amount of heat from the sun that Earth does. Why does Earth have oceans and an oxygen atmosphere while Venus is dry and hot? Could Venus be an example of a runaway greenhouse effect?

Hiking in the bog.   *Don DeMille photo.*

Chapter Thirteen

Take a Hike

Most of the 4,000 hectare Burns Bog is private property and is unfortunately closed to the public. But throughout the bog several areas are open to hikers. These accessible areas offer visitors a unique experience. Here within sight of one of the world's great cities lies a huge wilderness that, despite overwhelming pressure, manages to retain much of the wildness that makes it such a treasure.

There are three distinctly separate hiking areas in, around and near the bog. Map 1 shows where each of the areas is located. Map 2 illustrates access points to the public trails in the heart of the bog. And map 3 shows the Delta Nature Reserve trails and those in Watershed Park, which straddles the edge of the bog and uplands.

A word of caution: vehicles of any description are not welcome in any of these areas. Even bicycles are discouraged. So-called mountain bikes erode trails and cause severe damage to these delicate ecosystems. In some areas of the bog, irresponsible operators of all-terrain vehicles have gouged wide swaths into the bog's soft, peaty surface.

Recently, Watershed Park has become very popular with mountain bikers, especially on weekends. It's no fun to walk around a blind corner to meet a mountain biker hurtling toward you at 30 km per hour. Keep your head up and your eyes open.

That old adage still holds true: Take nothing but photos, leave nothing but footprints.

Hiking in the Bog

The area immediately north of the Burns Bog landfill (see map 2) is a favourite destination among hikers. Although bounded by the dump on the south and private properties on all other points of the compass, this region affords visitors a rare opportunity to experience a living, breathing bog.

Once hikers leave the main access roads and move into the interior trails, it is easy to disappear for hours in this breathtakingly beautiful wilderness.

The dotted grid lines shown north of the dump on map 2 are, in fact, surveyors' slashes cut into the bog vegetation. These cut-lines allow visitors to explore the area with relatively little danger of getting lost. The tall radio towers near 68th and 80th streets are also handy reference points, as is the giant Tilbury Cement plant on Tilbury Island in the north.

Each of the square grids represents a block approximately 200 metres square (except those immediately adjacent to the north side of the dump, which are approximately 400 metres north-south and 200 metres east-west).

While the grid system is a good way to design your own hiking circuit, always knowing where you are, give-or-take half a kilometre or so, keep in mind that the bog is a huge, wild area. Landmarks notwithstanding, it is a good idea to bring along a high-quality compass.

The Delta Nature Reserve trails shown on map 3 offer easy family hiking. Much of the area is boardwalked. Of special interest in this area is the derelict bulldozer. Its location is marked with a ✳ on map 3.

Watershed Park, also shown on map 3, offers a much different experience than the other areas. The upland or northeastern edge of the park feels far more like a West Coast rainforest than a bog.

Finally, the areas marked as private property on these maps should be respected as such.

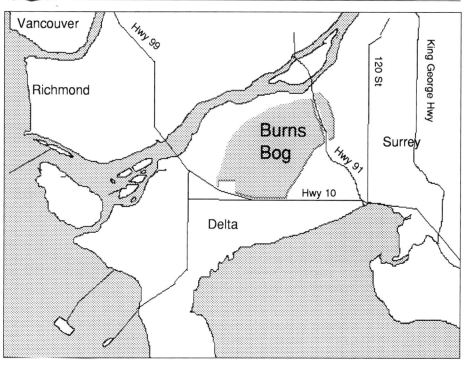

Vancouver

Richmond

Hwy 99

Burns
Bog

Delta

Surrey

120 St

King George Hwy

Hwy 91

Hwy 10

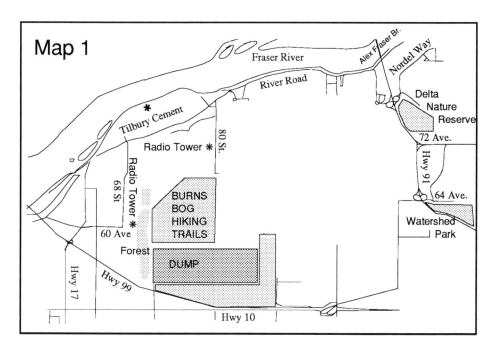

Map 1

Fraser River

Alex Fraser Br.

Nordel Way

River Road

Tilbury Cement

Delta
Nature
Reserve

72 Ave.

80 St.

Radio Tower ✳

Hwy 91

Radio Tower ✳

68 St

BURNS
BOG
HIKING
TRAILS

64 Ave.

60 Ave

Watershed
Park

Forest

DUMP

Hwy 17

Hwy 99

Hwy 10

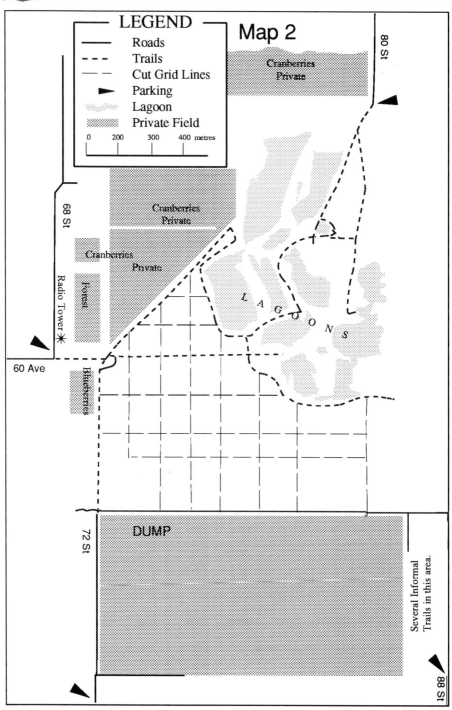

LEGEND

Map 2

— Roads
--- Trails
-- Cut Grid Lines
▶ Parking
Lagoon
Private Field

0   200   300   400 metres

80 St

Cranberries
Private

68 St

Cranberries
Private

Cranberries
Private

Radio Tower ✳

Forest

L A G O O N S

60 Ave

Blueberries

72 St

DUMP

Several Informal
Trails in this area.

88 St

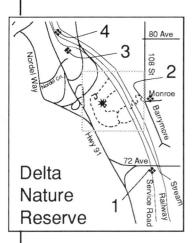

Delta Nature Reserve

Map 3
Access routes -
❖ Delta Nature Reserve
▲ Watershed Park

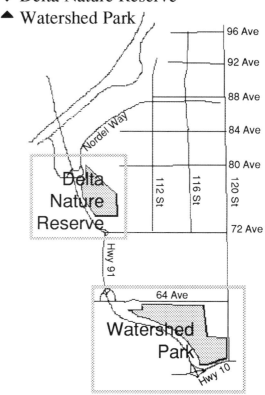

Access to Delta Nature Reserve

1. Hike north into the reserve along the service road from 72 Ave.

2. Hike into the reserve from the trailhead at 108 St. and Monroe.

3. Park at the Great Pacific Forum on Nordel Way, walk north to the service road, then follow it south into the reserve.

4. Park at the Sidetrack Pub on River Rd. and walk south along the service road into the reserve.

Access to Watershed Park

5. Easy access through many visible but unmarked points along 64 Ave. (Kittson Parkway) west of Wade Rd.

6. At west end of Pinewood at Pinewood School.

7. Under Hwy 10 just northeast of the junction with Hwy 91.

8. On the northbound lane of Hwy 91 halfway between Hwy 10 and 64 Ave., a truck pulloff affords easy access to the park.

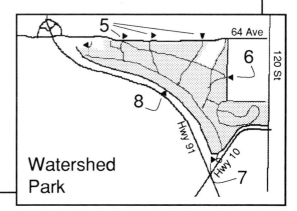

Burns Bog—What price wilderness?   *Don DeMille photo.*

Chapter Fourteen

Visions for the Future

"The purchase of Burns Bog would enhance ecotourism.
The old peat plant is the perfect spot for an ecomuseum."

Eliza Olson, president
Burns Bog Conservation Society

What lies in the future for Burns Bog? The fundamental question in this preserve-or-develop dilemma is whether the bog is worth saving. Dr. Richard Hebda states, "You will not find such a large self-contained raised bog with the same species anywhere else in the world. Burns Bog is an exceptional ecological treasure."

This appeal to save peatland for future generations rests on the premise that soils are our most precious resource. And we need wildland forever. David Suzuki says, "Burns Bog is one of a vanishing kind—a special bit of nature as it has been for millennia. It should be left completely alone."

Dr. David Bellamy, an authority on peat bogs, has visited almost all the major bogs on earth. He describes Burns Bog as "a unique raised bog that has already fought back from the brink of extinction, a thing of immense value and lasting utility and beauty. As the people of Vancouver ponder the way ahead, they should remember that whatever their decision, the results can be seen from outer space. What an epitaph to their stupidity or good sense."

As the largest undeveloped land mass in any major Canadian city, Burns Bog faces tremendous pressure. The City of Vancouver owns 627 hectares of the bog where it operates the second-largest landfill in Canada. Only part of the landfill is being used now, but with other regional dumps closing, the Burns Bog landfill will eventually expand.

Western Delta Lands ranks as the major private landholder in the bog. The company owns 2,300 of the 4,000 hectares of bog. After lengthy negotiations with WDL, the province's offer of $27.5 million was rejected in 1996 as being too low. Many years ago, WDL sought approval for a $10.5 billion port/city complex. Given the public outcry over the scale of the project, it is doubtful any other similar mega-projects will go forward.

Yet other large-scale developments continue to threaten Burns Bog. These include a proposed highway that will slice through the bog, and golf courses. Ironically, numerous smaller projects, including private landfills and the widening of existing roads, offer perhaps the greatest threat. These piecemeal projects slowly erode the fringes of the bog.

No one would deny the unique ecological nature of Burns Bog. Unfortunately, for many decision-makers and public figures the bottom line lies in the dollar value of Burns Bog. At first glance, the option of preserving Burns

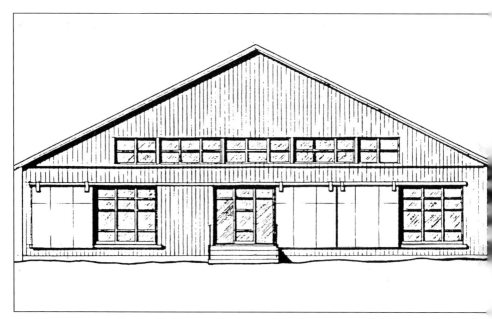

Architect Roxanne Button's drawings of a proposed interpretive centre for the Bog.

Bog suffers when compared to its development potential. Any large-scale development would create much-needed jobs. The huge size of the bog could accommodate thousands of houses. The proposal for a vast port/industrial/residential complex, which was defeated, would have housed 125,000 people. All these development options would generate tax dollars.

On the other side of the ledger, preserving the bog seems to offer little immediate return. Pro-bog development proponents concede that if the bog was saved, an interpretive centre could possibly generate tourist dollars. But the money would be nothing in comparison to the revenue the municipality could expect from the extra taxpayers if the bog were opened to a huge housing tract.

Looking beyond a dollar value, preserving Burns Bog offers a number of positive benefits. While these might seem valueless at first, in the long term these benefits could turn out to be the best investment for the future.

Consider one vital contribution that Burns Bog makes, namely the improvement of the region's air quality. By acting as the lungs of the Lower Mainland,

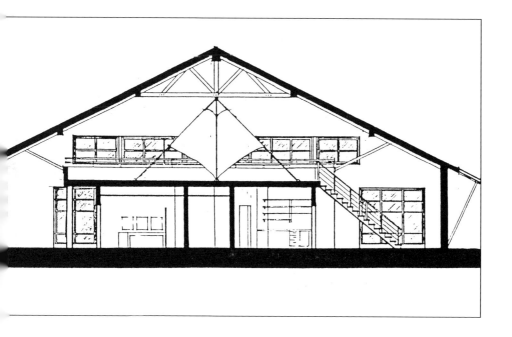

Burns Bog plays a positive role in maintaining air quality as well as cooling the air. No one has yet been able to assign an exact dollar value to clean air and no formula exists which accurately puts a price tag on the collective health of 2 million people.

However, a City of Vancouver program promoting tree planting estimates a single tree over 50 years will generate $30,000 worth of oxygen and recycle $35,000 worth of water as well as $60,000 worth of pollution cleanup.

Paul Heraty, spokesman for the tree planting program, says, "An acre of young trees can produce enough oxygen for 18 people."

Burns Bog, as an extensive peatland, operates as a "natural sink for atmospheric carbon dioxide and pollution. Wetlands have been called nature's kidneys because they function as filters... reducing the effects of pollution," according to Environment Canada.

According to the Wetland Ecosystem Research Group, an active bog is capable of accumulating up to the equivalent of 8 tonnes of carbon dioxide per hectare per year. This equals the annual emission of 2.25 average cars. Thus Burns Bog offsets the emissions from 9,000 cars each year.

While many dismiss bog tourism as not being a viable option, in reality this is an enormous growth industry. Ecotourism has boomed as the baby boomers slow down to smell the roses. Aging baby boomers enjoy passive activities such as trail walking, wildlife watching and bird watching. For a number of years bird watching was the fastest-growing outdoor activity in North America. Included within the broad sweep of the term ecotourism or adventure touring are bed-and-breakfast stays, river tours, photo hikes and guided tours of the bog.

These activities are "expanding at 15 percent a year, the fastest-growing segment of the tourist industry," according to a recent tourism study. Most of these tourists are North American long weekenders who spend an average of three days at one destination.

Ecotourists tend to be drawn by a specific destination activity, whether a three-day river rafting experience or a bike tour of the Gulf Islands. What would draw tourists to Burns Bog? An ecomuseum complex located in Burns Bog would offer tourists a destination. Such a complex would need a focus—something to draw people—or a single focal point.

Architect Roxanne Button designed an Environmental Education and Interpretive Centre with the Visions Committee of the Burns Bog Conservation Society.

To give the centre a focus, the plan revolved around using the deserted peat plant off Hwy 91 at the eastern end of the bog. Other successful tourist-museums use existing industrial buildings. The museum at Steveston is housed in an old fish plant. Granville Island utilizes old industrial buildings. Both are popular tourist spots.

The location of the old peat plant, which dates back to 1946, offers more than just a natural focus. Restoring and running the old railway on the existing rail lines through the bog would offer a unique ride back in history for eco-tourists. The line could terminate at the hovercraft rusting away on a huge pond.

The peat plant is located close to a major highway and connected to the Fraser River to the north and Boundary Bay to the south. While the original peat plant buildings have been demolished, rebuilding is one option. Another is erecting new structures. Or another site could be chosen.

Burns Bog needs preserving. This exceptional ecological treasure is more than just a unique raised bog. Functioning as the lungs and kidneys of the Lower Mainland, Burns Bog positively benefits both air quality and water quality. This

Burns Bog Conservation Society president Eliza Olson and naturalist David Bellamy.   *Bill Burns photo.*

The Living Museum

An ecomuseum is a living museum of the environment. The model proposed for Burns Bog incorporates education, research and recreation. Such a centre, no matter where it is located, should fulfill academic as well as community needs. Canada holds an extensive amount of the remaining world's peatlands, yet our country does not have a peatland research facility.

Other aspects of the ecomuseum complex include:

- The ecomuseum complex should be the centre of greenspace and a trail network linking the area between the Fraser River and Boundary Bay.

- This ecomuseum would focus on heritage preservation, both of the historical peat working and of First Nations archaeological wet sites along the Fraser.

- The building plans feature a nature interpretive centre that school tours could visit before or after their field trip to the bog and students could be shown samples of unique bog plants in a series of hands-on displays.

- Research labs would allow Burns Bog to become an international centre in peatland ecology, concentrating on biological and botanical research.

- A restored railway once used for peat farming would offer an unusual focus. The derelict hovercraft peat machine could also be restored.

- An extensive network of nature trails and boardwalks, as well as observation towers, would allow access to the bog and its wildlife and plant life.

- A gift shop and restaurant could feature food from the bog, including, of course, the bog's unique Labrador tea.

- Cottage industries such as harvesting Labrador tea, and artwork and crafts based on a Burns Bog theme could become an off-shoot of this centre.

contribution adds to the quality of life of all Lower Mainland residents. Health is something that is impossible to measure in monetary terms.

If the bog were saved by government intervention, building an ecomuseum would offer more than just an adjunct. Besides becoming a local destination, and adding tourist dollars to the area, Burns Bog could become a national or even international attraction should an educational/research centre be established.

Building such a centre would attract the very best in the field. One Canadian scientist has already expressed interest.

Heather Gill-Robinson, a former teacher, became interested in peat bogs when shown a picture of Tollund Man during an anthropology course. A photo of "a beautifully preserved Danish bog body over 2,000 years old," sparked her interest, "and that was it. I was hooked."

As Canada does not have suitable courses in her area, she had to go to England to study for her doctorate. She works under the supervision of Prof. Don Brothwell, an expert on the British Lindow Man body. After completing her thesis on the preservation of human and animal soft tissue in peat bogs, Gill-Robinson wants to return to Canada. She has expressed interest in doing research and possibly teaching at a Burns Bog ecocentre.

Other countries now recognize peatlands as extremely important to world health, especially as they help counterbalance global warming. Ireland has set up a Visitor Centre at a bog in County Mayo. Canada needs a peatland research centre and Burns Bog offers the ideal location, situated in the midst of a metropolis.

Acknowledgments

So many people helped with this book it is not possible to mention everyone. Bryan McGill's encouragement started me off and sustained me on this long and difficult project. Bryan edits *Beautiful BC* magazine, which published my feature article on Burns Bog in the winter 1995 issue. Over three years ago Don DeMille took me on my first hike on Burns Bog. My "guide" ended up as a friend. A remarkably talented man, both scientist and artist, Don opened my eyes to the beauty and uniqueness of Burns Bog. His contributions to this book go far beyond his photographs.

The author of over 40 books and 400 TV nature programs, David Bellamy spent his honeymoon on a bog and wants to be buried in one. His passion for and commitment to saving peatlands has landed him in jail for protesting against destruction of wetlands. I witnessed the private side of David, and found him an exceedingly patient and approachable man.

Dr. Richard Hebda of the Royal B.C. Museum generously helped in a number of ways: writing a foreword, setting aside time for interviews and assisting me with the complex scientific aspects of peatlands.

Eliza Olson of the Burns Bog Conservation Society provided not only encouragement, but valuable resources, names and information. The society's library and staff also helped with this book.

Many others shared their knowledge, including zoologist and bird expert Dr. Mary Taitt, semi-retired biology teacher Hollis Kelly, hunter Gary Biggar and F. Farrell, who grew up next to the bog and spent many days doing research on Dominic Burns. Through her, I discovered Dominic Burns' last name was originally O'Byrne, the same last name as that of my forbears. In an even stranger coincidence, both O'Byrnes left Ireland for Canada in the same year, 1848, although my family came from a different county. As O'Byrne is the seventh-most-common Irish name, I doubt I'm related.

Although a number of experts helped with this book, any errors are entirely mine.

Initially a number of B.C. publishers expressed interest in the book. But one after another, all the publishers backed out, concerned with "profitability." Hugh Wilson at Hurricane Press saw beyond the balance sheet and rescued the project.

What sustained me over the years was not only the support of all these people, but the bog itself. Moments stand out in my memory.

David Bellamy playfully dove into a lagoon on a hike on Burns Bog. Within minutes others joined him in a huge outdoor peat pool.

While interviewing Mary Taitt at her residence at Reifel, the two resident sandhill cranes flapped into the air and circled the house, providing a magic moment.

I recall Don DeMille and his mother showing me their "secret" blueberry patch where they picked berries for almost 25 years. Later I started my own family tradition by taking my daughter Danielle to the same area. But she refused to let me pick any bush clean, scolding, "Dad! Leave some blueberries for the bears." Her concern for wildlife made me proud.

Our children are not only our most valuable resource, they will hopefully better protect our dwindling natural resources.

Bill Burns
Surrey, B.C.

Index

Plants and animals are listed under their English names. Page numbers for photographs and artwork are in *italics*.

Leach, Barry, 21
leachate, 92–97
Lebans, Tanya, 95
Les, John, 88
Lindow Man, 64–71, 121
Lindow Woman, 65
Lortie, Norm, 86
Luckman, Brian, 106

McDonald, Bruce, 85
MacEwan, Grant, 77
McGill, Bryan, 122
Mackenzie, William, 77
mammals in Burns Bog, 12, 34–35
mariposa copper butterfly, 10, 35, *46*
marsh, 17
Marshall, David, 26
megaport proposal, 10, 83, 116, 117
merlins, 37
metals contamination, 24, 92, 96
methane, 12
mice, 34
monarch butterfly, *46*
Moorhead, Fiona, 97
muskrat, *33, 34*
Musqueam people, 76, 87, 89

newt, 26
Newton, Amy, 97
northern harrier, *38*
northwest salamander, *34*

O'Byrne family, 76, 122
Olson, Eliza, 4–5, 10, 84, 115, *119,* 122
organism, 7
owls, 34, 37, *38*
ozone, 101, 105–107

Pacific Flyway, 12, 37, 40
Pacific tree frog, *33*
peat
  as catalytic agent, 79

formation of, 17, 104
harvesting of, in Canada, 50, 78–79, *81*
railway, 62, 79, 119
power plants using, 49–50
uses of, 49–50
peatlands
  definition of, 10
  European, 10–11, 50, 65. *See also*
    Ireland, bogs of
  importance of, 17–18
  as natural archives, 4, 69–70
  storage of carbon, 17–18. *See also* carbon sink
peregrine falcon, 34
Pitt River, 41
Point Roberts, 23–24, 40
pollen, 69–70
pollution, 24, 26, 92–96, 99–107, 118
population, 25, *82,* 92, 99, 105
porcupine, *33,* 34

rabbit, *32*
raccoon, *32,* 34
railway in Burns Bog, 62, 79, 119
raised-dome bog, 4, 48, 104–105, 115
RAMSAR site, 40
raptors, 12, 24, 37
recreation in Burns Bog. *See* hiking trails
red fox, *32,* 34
redtailed hawk, 37, *41*
reptiles, 34–35
ring-necked pheasant, *38*
Roberts, Capt. Henry, 23
Romanov family, 68–69
Romans, 65–66
rough-legged hawks, 37
Royal B.C. Museum, 11, 17
Rusk, Allan, 60
Russia, bogs of, 10, 49

salal, *46*
salamander, 26

Postscript

A Message from the Burns Bog Conservation Society

Dear Reader,

I founded the Burns Bog Conservation Society in 1988 with nine other people after the deepsea port megaproject was defeated. We knew even then that we had won the battle but not the war to protect Burns Bog. We also knew that we would have to be prepared to fight any new proposals to destroy Burns Bog. This could only be done by raising public awareness; Bill's book is one of the results of our educational campaign.

The effort to save Burns Bog is not over. This is why your support is so important. Letters need to be written and books need to be purchased for our library. Staff need to conduct tours, build boardwalks, service our members and work with volunteers.

Your support is so terribly urgent because, even as I write this, plans are being made to diminish and ultimately destroy Burns Bog.

Our job will not be finished even when Burns Bog receives the protection it so richly deserves. The research/interpretive centre must still be built. We'll need wardens and interpretive guides to work with the public and researchers to study the bog.

You can help. As a first step, please join or contribute to our Society which is dedicated to the preservation of Burns Bog. Get to know this amazing place. Bring your friends and your children because I suspect the effort required to save it will be multigenerational. The sooner we hear from you, the sooner we can put your contribution to work protecting the Bog.

Eliza Olson, President